PRAISE FOR THE PREVIOUSLY PUBLISHED
VISUAL THEOLOGY: SEEING AND UNDERSTANDING THE TRUTH ABOUT GOD

Tim Challies (the writer) and Josh Byers (the designer) have teamed up to produce a truly unique introduction to theology and guide to living the Christian life. This is show-and-tell at its finest. Most theology books merely convey what we are to believe, but this one uses creative and beautiful design to capture and portray these crucial truths. I know of nothing else quite like it, and I trust that God will use it to help his people see and celebrate reality in a new way.

JUSTIN TAYLOR, managing editor of the *ESV Study Bible* and coauthor of *The Final Days of Jesus*

This is simple yet profound, clever without being flashy. Helpful and practical. Speaking as a person who avoids diagrams and graphs at all costs, I found the infographics in this book to be illuminating. This cheeky little number is a class act.

MEZ MCCONNELL, pastor of Niddrie Community Church, Edinburgh, and director of 20schemes

You've probably seen (or used) a gospel presentation drawn on a whiteboard or a napkin. It's remarkable how God gives us spiritual insight when we behold truths about him with our eyes. With engaging graphics and descriptions of the Christian faith, Tim Challies and Josh Byers have done something genuinely unique in *Visual Theology*. See for yourself!

GLORIA FURMAN, author of *Treasuring Christ When Your Hands Are Full* and *The Pastor's Wife*

My mind is blown. Tim Challies and Josh Byers marry rock-ribbed Reformational theology with breathtaking presentations. The effect is something like following John Knox into the Matrix. In this diaphanous world, we encounter no fiction, but very reality itself — God-reality — and we are transformed.

OWEN STRACHAN, associate professor of Christian theology and director of the Center on Gospel and Culture at Midwestern Baptist Theological Seminary

A VISUAL THEOLOGY

GUIDE
TO THE
BIBLE

SEEING AND **KNOWING**
GOD'S WORD

A VISUAL THEOLOGY

GUIDE
TO THE
BIBLE

SEEING AND **KNOWING**
GOD'S WORD

TIM CHALLIES and **JOSH BYERS**

with JOEY SCHWARTZ

ZONDERVAN

A Visual Theology Guide to the Bible
Copyright © 2019 by Tim Challies and Josh Byers

ISBN 978-0-310-57796-6 (softcover)

Requests for information should be addressed to:
Zondervan, *3900 Sparks Dr. SE, Grand Rapids, Michigan 49546*

Published in association with the literary agency of Wolgemuth & Associates, Inc.

Cover design: Studio Gearbox
Interior design and illustrations: Josh Byers

Printed in the United States of America

19 20 21 22 23 24 25 26 27 /WPW/ 15 14 13 12 11 10 9 8 7 6 5 4 3 2 1

CONTENTS

Introduction _____ 8

PART 1: TRUSTING THE BIBLE

1. What Is the Bible? _____ 14
2. How Was the Bible Written? _____ 25
3. How Were the Books Collected? _____ 35
4. What Makes the Bible Unique? _____ 50
5. Can We Trust the Bible? _____ 60

PART 2: STUDYING THE BIBLE

6. Why Should I Study the Bible? _____ 74
7. How Do I Study the Bible? _____ 84

PART 3: SEEING THE BIBLE

8. What Is the Bible About? _____ 102
9. Creation, Fall, & Flood: The Need for Jesus _____ 109
10. Abraham, Moses, & the Law: The Foundation for Jesus _____ 116
11. Land, Judges, & Kings: Preparation for Jesus _____ 132
12. Songs & Wisdom: The Longing for Jesus _____ 144
13. Prophets, Exile, & a New Covenant: Expectation of Jesus _____ 156
14. The Gospel & the Kingdom: The Coming of Jesus _____ 168
15. Pentecost & the Early Church: Continuation of Jesus _____ 180
16. The Apostles, Exiles, & the End: The Commands of Jesus & Consummation in Jesus ___ 190

Conclusion _____ 200

Acknowledgments _____ 201

Notes _____ 202

When it comes to books that stick around, none can match the Bible. Its words have been treasured through the ages, committed to memory, printed in scrolls, bound in books, narrated on tape, and programmed in apps. When it comes to books that sell, the Bible stands apart. Year after year, its sales skyrocket past the hottest *New York Times* bestsellers. When it comes to books with influence, the Bible is equally unique, its fingerprints manifest in the laws and constitutions of great nations, in key literary works and defining treatises. In endurance, influence, and sales, all other books pale in comparison.[1]

IN THE UNITED STATES ALONE

AN ESTIMATED
40,000,000
COPIES ARE SOLD YEARLY

82%
OF ALL HOUSEHOLDS HAVE AT LEAST ONE BIBLE

72%
HAVE MULTIPLE

13%
OF ALL PEOPLE PURCHASE A BIBLE EACH YEAR

52%
OF AMERICANS SAY THEY READ THE BIBLE 3-4 TIMES PER YEAR

THE *FULL* BIBLE IS AVAILABLE IN

670

DIFFERENT LANGUAGES

THIS GIVES

5,371,000,000

PEOPLE ACCESS TO THE ENTIRE BIBLE

THE NEW TESTAMENT IS AVAILABLE IN

1,521

ADDITIONAL LANGUAGES

GIVING

658,000,000

ADDITIONAL PEOPLE ACCESS

BUT TO CHRISTIANS, THE BIBLE IS MORE THAN
A CULTURAL ARTIFACT OR A LITERARY CURIOSITY.

TO CHRISTIANS, THE BIBLE IS DIVINE REVELATION
GOD'S MESSAGE TO THE WORLD.

IT UNVEILS THE MIND OF GOD

REVEALS THE WILL OF GOD

DESCRIBES THE WORK OF GOD

CALLS THE READER TO FAITH IN GOD

The Bible tells us who we are, why we exist, why we are so messy, how we are to relate to God, and how everything will someday be made right. It is reliable when it describes past events, theological when it describes divine truths, and inspirational when it calls for a heartfelt response.

The Bible makes monumental claims about itself. It describes itself as light to guide the lost, medicine to revive the sick, wisdom to correct the foolish, inspiration to cheer the sorrowful, balm to heal the blind. It insists it is more valuable than gold and sweeter than honey. It declares it is able to teach truth and correct error, that it will guide us away from unethical behavior and toward behavior that serves and blesses others.

A host of key historical figures attest to the Bible's unique significance. England's Queen Elizabeth II asked, "To what greater inspiration and counsel can we turn than to the imperishable truth to be found in this treasure house, the Bible?"[2] Abraham Lincoln declared, "[The Bible] is the best gift God has given to man. All the good the Saviour gave to the world was communicated through this book. But for it we could not know right from wrong."[3] Far above the world's greatest leaders and powers and institutions stands the timeless wisdom of the Bible.

This is a book about the Bible, and especially what the Bible contains. We have prepared it as enthusiasts who love the Bible, who attempt to understand it rightly and obey it truly. We have prepared it as pastors who love people and long to help them discover how the Bible answers their toughest questions and satisfies their deepest longings. We have prepared it as Christians, who have banked all we have and all we are on the Bible's great claims. We have prepared it as partners—an author and an artist—who each bring our individual passion to bear, one in the medium of words and the other in the medium of art.

If you are new to the Bible, we hope to motivate you to explore it for yourself, to read some of its key passages, to consider its claims, and to understand its most important themes. We will guide you from the beginning to the end to show how its many authors, hundreds of characters, and thousands of chapters together narrate one grand story that makes sense of this world and establishes your place in it.

If you are experienced with the Bible, we hope to motivate you to explore the Bible again, to read it with clearer eyes, and to come to a deeper appreciation of its central themes and supernatural cohesion. We know you will enjoy reading about this sacred Book and studying the graphics that illustrate it.

Whether you've read the Bible through a hundred times or have never read a single word, we invite you to join us as we describe and display the most important, most influential, most popular, and most life-changing book the world has ever known. Come and meet the Bible—or meet it all over again.

CHAPTER ONE

WHAT IS THE BIBLE?

What Christians call "the Bible" or "the Holy Bible" isn't the only bible in the world, is it? Browse your local bookstore and you'll find all kinds of books with the word *bible* in the title. A quick search turns up *The Furniture Bible*, a guide to identifying, restoring, and caring for antique furniture; *The Metal Detecting Bible*, the definitive guide for discovering lost valuables; and the *Jeep Owner's Bible*, a guide for getting the most out of your Jeep. From these examples we see that employing the word *bible* represents a claim of authority. A bible is an authoritative source of wisdom or knowledge. The implication is that you can't properly restore furniture without *The Furniture Bible*, and you can't hope to tap every strength of your Jeep unless you read the *Jeep Owner's Bible*.

The word *bible* is derived from the ancient Greek word *biblos*, which refers not to a particular book but to the papyrus used to create an early form of paper. Soon the meaning of that word had been broadened to describe a book or scroll and then narrowed to refer to a sacred book or scroll. The word found its way into Latin and other European languages. Eventually, it came to refer to one particular book—the Christian Bible. There may be a *Jeep Owner's Bible* and a *Metal Detecting Bible*, but there is only one Bible that needs no further explanation or qualification. And when we do wish to qualify it, we add the word *holy*, which means the Bible is set apart, a book unlike any other.

So, what is this Bible? Let's begin to answer that question by looking at the Bible's structure and purpose.

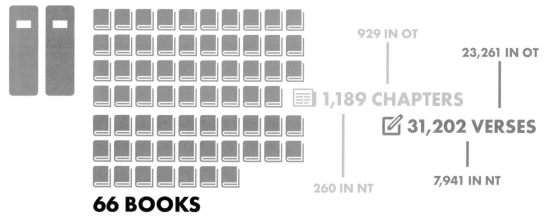

2 TESTAMENTS

66 BOOKS

929 IN OT

260 IN NT

1,189 CHAPTERS

23,261 IN OT

7,941 IN NT

31,202 VERSES

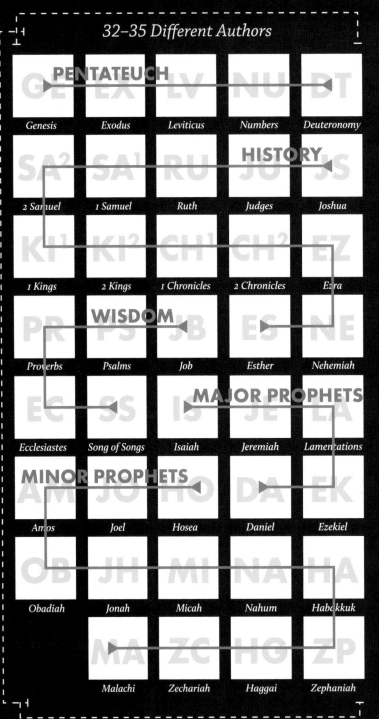

32–35 Different Authors

Old Testament – 39 Books

PENTATEUCH

GE	EX	LV	NU	DT
Genesis	Exodus	Leviticus	Numbers	Deuteronomy

HISTORY

SA²	SA¹	RU	JU	JS
2 Samuel	1 Samuel	Ruth	Judges	Joshua

KI¹	KI²	CH¹	CH²	EZ
1 Kings	2 Kings	1 Chronicles	2 Chronicles	Ezra

WISDOM

PR	PS	JB	ES	NE
Proverbs	Psalms	Job	Esther	Nehemiah

MAJOR PROPHETS

EC	SS	IS	JE	LA
Ecclesiastes	Song of Songs	Isaiah	Jeremiah	Lamentations

MINOR PROPHETS

AM	JO	HO	DA	EK
Amos	Joel	Hosea	Daniel	Ezekiel

OB	JH	MI	NA	HA
Obadiah	Jonah	Micah	Nahum	Habakkuk

MA	ZC	HG	ZP
Malachi	Zechariah	Haggai	Zephaniah

Written approximately 1446–400 BC

76% of the Bible

WHAT IS THE STRUCTURE OF THE BIBLE?

The Bible is much like any other book in that it has internal cohesion. From beginning to end, it provides a unified picture of who God is, who we are, and what we need most. It is not merely a collection of words, sayings, and stories tossed together, but information that has been carefully collected and placed within a structure. The Bible moves from descriptions of the most distant past to predictions of a coming future. As it does that, it tells the story of humanity and the God who created us.[1]

TESTAMENTS

Its broadest structure is a division into two "Testaments," the Old Testament and the New Testament. The word we translate as "testament" could more accurately be translated as "covenant," so when we speak of Old Testament and New Testament, we are really speaking of Old Covenant and New Covenant. A covenant is an agreement between two parties that governs the terms of their relationship. The Old Testament details the establishment of the Old Covenant and the promises of the coming Christ, and the New Testament describes the inauguration of the New Covenant that God had planned all along. This shows why the Bible is divided in this way. The Old Testament includes all those parts of the Bible that were completed before the birth and death of Jesus Christ, and the New Testament includes all those parts of the Bible that were completed after his birth and death.

BOOKS

Each of the Testaments is made up of what we call "books." This is perhaps not the most helpful term, since some of these "books" are actually letters, some are collections of songs and poetry, and some are only a few hundred words long. Still, that's the word that has stuck. There are thirty-nine books in the Old Testament and twenty-seven in the New Testament for a total of sixty-six. The Old Testament composes roughly three-quarters of the Bible, and the New Testament approximately

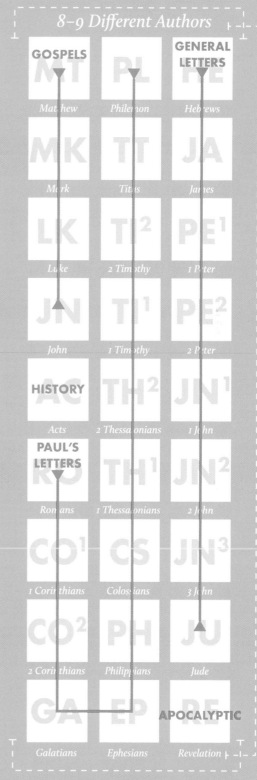

New Testament – 27 Books

Written approximately AD 45–95
24% of the Bible

one-quarter. The Old Testament books tell of the creation of the world, the founding of the Israelites, the establishment of those people in the promised land, their special relationship with God, their disobedience to God, and their resulting captivity by hostile nations. A constant theme is the promise of a Messiah who will fully and finally liberate the Israelites from danger and oppression. The New Testament books tell of the birth, life, and death of Jesus; they tell of the work of the earliest Christians to spread their message; they instruct Christians in how to live and tell how God intends to bring history to its close. A recurring theme is that Jesus is the Messiah who was promised in the Old Testament.

NAMES

Each of the books in the Bible has a name. The books were not often given names at the time they were written, so they took them on over time as people read and studied them. They are often named after the author of the book or after one of its key characters. Thus, Isaiah is both by and about a prophet named Isaiah; Luke is an account of the

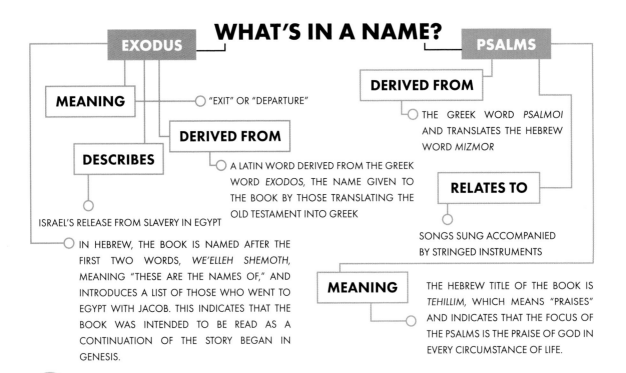

A VISUAL THEOLOGY GUIDE TO THE BIBLE

life of Jesus written by an early Christian historian named Luke. Sometimes books are given a name that summarizes their content. Genesis describes the genesis, or beginning, of the world and of God's chosen people, the Israelites; Psalms contains a collection of songs of worship known as psalms; Acts describes the acts of the earliest Christians. The New Testament letters are usually titled according to the recipient, though sometimes they are titled according to the sender. Ephesians is Paul's letter to the church in Ephesus; 1 Timothy is Paul's first of two letters to his protégé, Timothy; 2 John is John's second of three letters to an unspecified church.[2]

CHAPTERS AND VERSES

Books are divided into chapters, and chapters are divided into verses. These divisions were not present when the books were written but were added much later to assist with finding a specific place within the Bible. Today you may see a reference like John 3:16. John is the name of the book, 3 is the chapter, and 16 is the verse. Thus you could open your Bible to the book of John, turn to chapter three and verse 16 to find what may be the best-loved sentence in the entire Bible.

BOOK NAME — VERSE •

JOHN 3:16

CHAPTER —

The chapter divisions commonly used today were developed by Stephen Langton, an archbishop of Canterbury. Langton put the modern chapter divisions into place in around AD 1227.

The Hebrew Old Testament was divided into verses by a Jewish rabbi by the name of Nathan in AD 1448.

Robert Estienne, who was also known as Stephanus, was the first to divide the New Testament into standard numbered verses in AD 1555.

GENRES

If you visit a bookstore today and browse around, you'll find books divided into genres—books of different styles or with different purposes: historical novels, home decorating, modern history, and so on. Likewise, the biblical books fall into a number of genres. They include:

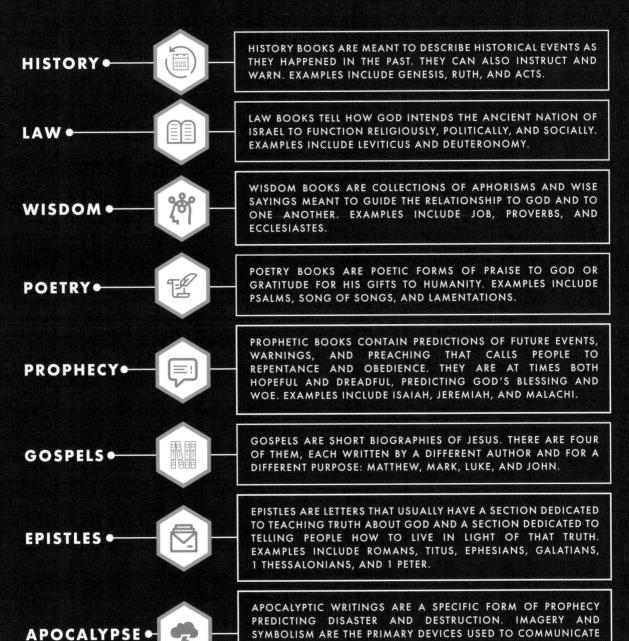

HISTORY — HISTORY BOOKS ARE MEANT TO DESCRIBE HISTORICAL EVENTS AS THEY HAPPENED IN THE PAST. THEY CAN ALSO INSTRUCT AND WARN. EXAMPLES INCLUDE GENESIS, RUTH, AND ACTS.

LAW — LAW BOOKS TELL HOW GOD INTENDS THE ANCIENT NATION OF ISRAEL TO FUNCTION RELIGIOUSLY, POLITICALLY, AND SOCIALLY. EXAMPLES INCLUDE LEVITICUS AND DEUTERONOMY.

WISDOM — WISDOM BOOKS ARE COLLECTIONS OF APHORISMS AND WISE SAYINGS MEANT TO GUIDE THE RELATIONSHIP TO GOD AND TO ONE ANOTHER. EXAMPLES INCLUDE JOB, PROVERBS, AND ECCLESIASTES.

POETRY — POETRY BOOKS ARE POETIC FORMS OF PRAISE TO GOD OR GRATITUDE FOR HIS GIFTS TO HUMANITY. EXAMPLES INCLUDE PSALMS, SONG OF SONGS, AND LAMENTATIONS.

PROPHECY — PROPHETIC BOOKS CONTAIN PREDICTIONS OF FUTURE EVENTS, WARNINGS, AND PREACHING THAT CALLS PEOPLE TO REPENTANCE AND OBEDIENCE. THEY ARE AT TIMES BOTH HOPEFUL AND DREADFUL, PREDICTING GOD'S BLESSING AND WOE. EXAMPLES INCLUDE ISAIAH, JEREMIAH, AND MALACHI.

GOSPELS — GOSPELS ARE SHORT BIOGRAPHIES OF JESUS. THERE ARE FOUR OF THEM, EACH WRITTEN BY A DIFFERENT AUTHOR AND FOR A DIFFERENT PURPOSE: MATTHEW, MARK, LUKE, AND JOHN.

EPISTLES — EPISTLES ARE LETTERS THAT USUALLY HAVE A SECTION DEDICATED TO TEACHING TRUTH ABOUT GOD AND A SECTION DEDICATED TO TELLING PEOPLE HOW TO LIVE IN LIGHT OF THAT TRUTH. EXAMPLES INCLUDE ROMANS, TITUS, EPHESIANS, GALATIANS, 1 THESSALONIANS, AND 1 PETER.

APOCALYPSE — APOCALYPTIC WRITINGS ARE A SPECIFIC FORM OF PROPHECY PREDICTING DISASTER AND DESTRUCTION. IMAGERY AND SYMBOLISM ARE THE PRIMARY DEVICES USED TO COMMUNICATE THEIR TRUTH. EXAMPLES INCLUDE DANIEL AND REVELATION.

WHAT IS THE PURPOSE OF THE BIBLE?

One of history's most influential Christian theologians began his magnum opus with this sentence: "Nearly all the wisdom we possess, that is to say, true and sound wisdom, consists of two parts: the knowledge of God and of ourselves."[3] When he spoke of "wisdom," he was not referring to mere facts and stats, to the kind of trivia that might create a *Jeopardy* winner. He was not referring to only the kind of life lessons that may be passed down from a grandfather to a grandson. He was referring to something much greater and much more significant. Properly understood, wisdom is knowledge of the world as it really is. It is a correct knowledge of who God is and who we are in relation to him. And further, it is an understanding of how we are to live accordingly. In that way wisdom is not mere knowledge, but knowledge that has been deliberately put into action.

The Bible exists to impart true and sound wisdom from God to humanity. It is through the Bible that we come to a correct knowledge of God and of ourselves.

If we are to properly understand ourselves, we need knowledge that comes from outside ourselves. If we are to properly understand this world, we need knowledge that comes from outside this world. The Bible is the source of that knowledge. It is God's revelation of himself.

In chapter 8, we will say much more about the grand story of the Bible. But for now, it's important to know that the purpose of the Bible is to show mankind who God is and his plan to save mankind from their sin through his Son, Jesus Christ.

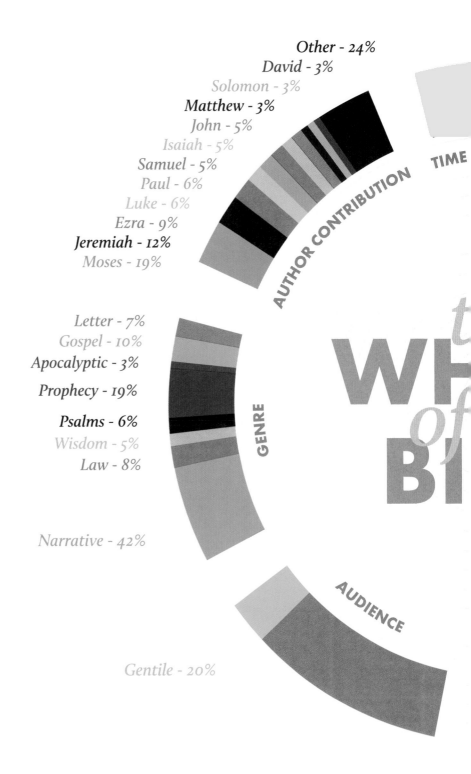

Other - 24%
David - 3%
Solomon - 3%
Matthew - 3%
John - 5%
Isaiah - 5%
Samuel - 5%
Paul - 6%
Luke - 6%
Ezra - 9%
Jeremiah - 12%
Moses - 19%

AUTHOR CONTRIBUTION

TIME

Letter - 7%
Gospel - 10%
Apocalyptic - 3%
Prophecy - 19%
Psalms - 6%
Wisdom - 5%
Law - 8%

GENRE

Narrative - 42%

AUDIENCE

Gentile - 20%

Israelite/Jewish - 80%

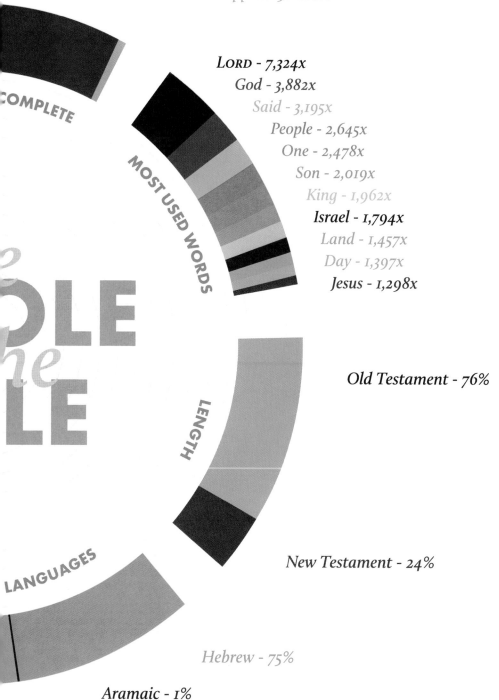

Old Testament - approx. 1,046 Years

New Testament - approx. 50 Years

COMPLETE

MOST USED WORDS

LORD - 7,324x
God - 3,882x
Said - 3,195x
People - 2,645x
One - 2,478x
Son - 2,019x
King - 1,962x
Israel - 1,794x
Land - 1,457x
Day - 1,397x
Jesus - 1,298x

Old Testament - 76%

LENGTH

New Testament - 24%

LANGUAGES

Hebrew - 75%

Aramaic - 1%

Greek - 24%

THE BIBLE IS GOD'S GIFT TO YOU

ONE COLLECTION

TWO TESTAMENTS

66 BOOKS

WRITTEN, ASSEMBLED, & PRESERVED

SO THAT YOU MIGHT KNOW HIM AND HIS SALVATION IN JESUS CHRIST.

CHAPTER TWO

HOW WAS THE BIBLE WRITTEN?

AS AN ARTIFACT, THE BIBLE HAS BEEN PRESERVED AND PRESENTED IN A VARIETY OF WAYS THROUGHOUT HISTORY

IT HAS TAKEN FORM IN WRITING, PRINTING, & CODE

In the dark corners of jail, the apostle Paul pens a letter to the church at Philippi. Through tears, he commands the church to rejoice in suffering and live in unity. After writing his final line, which would eventually be translated into English as "the grace of the Lord Jesus Christ be with your spirit," he drops his pen and prays.

Nearly two thousand years later, a teenage boy sits down in church, pulls out his iPhone, clicks on the "Bible" app, and scrolls down to the bottom of Philippians. As the preacher reads, he follows along: "The grace of our Lord Jesus Christ be with your spirit."

How did these words get from Paul's calloused hands into a twenty-first century smartphone? For that matter, how did all sixty-six of the ancient letters and books within the Bible survive into the present day?

The Bible was not delivered to us from the sky. It did not come to us fully formed from the hands of an angel. The Bible came from men who wrote the words of God. It was communicated in ancient languages, and it was preserved over the centuries. And yet, while the Bible is a historical artifact, we can be confident that the Bible we have today is far more: it is the very words of God.

THE BIBLE WAS GOD-BREATHED

In 2 Timothy 3:16, Paul writes to his protégé, "All Scripture is God-breathed and is useful for teaching, rebuking, correcting and training in righteousness." This beautiful imagery shows that all of the holy Scriptures (*graphē*) are spoken out by God, so that every word comes from his breath. This is why it's no stretch to read a passage of Scripture with the preface, "God says . . ." If it's in the Bible, then God spoke it, and he continues to speak those words into the lives of his children today (Hebrews 4:12).[1]

STONE & POTTERY PIECES

Inscriptions were carved or chiseled on blocks of broken pottery, loose stone, or larger edifices.

CLAY TABLETS

Clay was inscribed while it was still damp or soft. It would then be dried in the sun or baked in a kiln.

PAPYRI

Papyrus was made by pressing and gluing two layers of split papyrus reeds to form a sheet.

ANIMAL SKIN SCROLLS

Animal skin scrolls were made from the hides of calves, deer, sheep, goats, and cows.

This characteristic of Scripture is often called *inspiration*, although the term has become so muddled in modern usage that *God-breathed* may be a better term. The Old Testament prophets and the disciples were certainly not "inspired" in the same way that a country music star is "inspired" to write her hit song. The word *inspired* today has come to connote a vague influence, but Scripture is not just influenced by God. Scripture is spoken by God.

─ PRINTING ─

1456

PRINTED BOOKS

Johannes Gutenberg invented an improved printing press with metal movable type. The first volume printed on this improved press was the Gutenberg Bible.

─ CODING ─

1982

COMPUTER PROGRAMS

Verse Search was the first commercial Bible program developed by "THE WORD processor" family, Kent Ochel and Bert Brown, at Bible Research Systems.

1993

WEB PAGES

Bible Gateway was started in 1993 by Nick Hengeveld, a student at Calvin College in Grand Rapids, Michigan.

2008

APPS

Life Church released the YouVersion Bible App on the iPhone in 2008.

2016

VIRTUAL REALITY

VR Church launched Virtual Reality Bible and Church in 2016. It allows the wearer to view and browse virtual 3-D text in front of them.

─ BIOTECH ─

?

NEURAL DOWNLOADS

While not yet possible, scientists theorize in the future we'll be able to implant information directly into the brain and memory.

How were the Scriptures God-breathed? There are some instances when God audibly dictated words to a prophet or apostle, which were then recorded word for word (Isaiah 38:4–6; Revelation 2:1, 8, 12). But in many cases, it's unclear exactly how God spoke through his prophets. As the author of Hebrews notes, God spoke through his prophets "in various ways" (Hebrews 1:1).

In most cases, God didn't simply dictate his Word and employ the prophet or author as a scribe. God usually breathed out his Word using the personality, style, and circumstances of the author. Luke, for example, wrote his gospel using historical research, eyewitness interviews, and orderly reporting—and yet, Paul quotes the gospel of Luke as holy Scripture (1 Timothy 5:18). Paul himself wrote the Word of God out of the anguish of suffering and persecution (Ephesians 6:20; Colossians 4:18; 2 Timothy 2:9).

God ordained and oversaw the personality of the authors, their circumstances, their style, their training, and their process of writing to bring about his Word. The human authors were really writing, and God was really breathing.

THE BIBLE WAS HUMANLY COMMUNICATED

While the Bible is from God, it is for humans. God breathed out his Word to communicate with us. This means that God chose written words in human language as his primary way of speaking to us. The Bible was written in two primary languages—Hebrew and Greek—and one secondary language, Aramaic.

Almost all of the Old Testament was originally written in Hebrew. Coming from the Semitic family of languages, Hebrew was spoken and written by God's people, the Israelites, until around the third century BC.

While most of the Scriptures are written in Hebrew and Greek, Aramaic also plays a significant role in the Scriptures. Aramaic place names appear throughout the Old Testament, and three extended passages of Aramaic appear in the books of Daniel and Ezra.[2]

Aramaic is perhaps most significant because it was the most likely spoken language of Jesus and his disciples.[3] While Greek was used in writing because of its universal understanding, there is no doubt that the incarnate Lord and the apostles spoke in Aramaic, as is clear in the use of the Aramaic words "Cephas," "Matthew," "Abba," and "Maranatha." Most memorably, Jesus cried in Aramaic on the cross: *"Eli, Eli, lema sabachthani?"*[4]

The world into which Jesus was born was especially prepared for the spread of the gospel and the Scriptures. Alexander the Great's conquests from Greece to India had spread Greek culture and language across the globe so that by the New Testament era, Greek was spoken throughout the entire Mediterranean.

While Hebrew was a language used mostly by the people of Israel, Greek was the language for all people. As God extended his covenant promises to all nations and commanded his people to proclaim good news to the ends of the earth, the language of his written word shifted to accommodate this transition.[5] For the gospel to go to all nations, it had to be understood by all nations, and to be understood by the people of all nations, it was written in Greek.

It's important to note that the New Testament authors often quote and make use of the Septuagint, a Greek translation of the Old Testament, rather than the Hebrew Scriptures. This shows that while the biblical languages are significant, it was always expected that they would be translated into various languages so that all people could understand it. As John Frame writes, "The Bible does not assume that God's Word is untranslatable. Rather (in keeping with the nature of Christianity as a missionary religion), the Bible itself uses multiple languages."[6] God spoke his very words into Greek, Hebrew, and Aramaic through the biblical authors so that he could speak to us in our language today.

THE BIBLE WAS CAREFULLY PRESERVED

But how can we know that the Bible that God breathed out and that men recorded has been accurately preserved for us? How can we be sure that God's Word has remained God's Word from the time it was first written to this present day?

THE PRESERVATION OF THE OLD TESTAMENT

While recent scholarship has questioned the preservation of the original manuscripts of the Bible, the truth is that the

Bible has more evidence for its integrity than any other ancient book.[7] Recent archaeological findings confirm the faithfulness of the Bible we have in our possession.

In 1946, a Bedouin shepherd discovered a handful of ancient scrolls in the caves of Qumran. A deeper search over the next two years led to the finding of the Dead Sea Scrolls, the greatest manuscript discovery of the modern era.[8] Archaeologists found thousands of biblical fragments dating back to as early as the second century BC, including the entire book of Isaiah and pieces of every Old Testament book except Esther.[9]

Before the discovery of the Dead Sea Scrolls, biblical scholars had to rely on the ninth century AD Masoretic Text in order to translate the original Hebrew manuscripts into

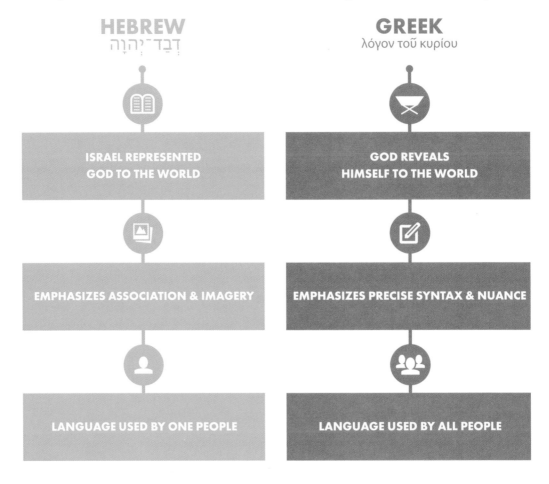

HEBREW	GREEK
דְּבַד־יְהֹוָה	λόγον τοῦ κυρίου
ISRAEL REPRESENTED GOD TO THE WORLD	GOD REVEALS HIMSELF TO THE WORLD
EMPHASIZES ASSOCIATION & IMAGERY	EMPHASIZES PRECISE SYNTAX & NUANCE
LANGUAGE USED BY ONE PEOPLE	LANGUAGE USED BY ALL PEOPLE

other languages. The Dead Sea Scrolls gave scholars a fresh opportunity to compare much earlier manuscripts with the Masoretic Text.

Many of the scrolls demonstrated a striking similarity to the Masoretic Text. In the book of Isaiah, for example, the Dead Sea Scrolls lined up exactly about 95 percent of the time. The 5 percent of differences between the two texts were primarily the result of obvious scribal errors.

What is the significance of this? It serves as just one of many evidences that over the course of many centuries, the Hebrew text was preserved. Because of the similarities in the manuscript, we can be confident that the Old Testament we have today is an extremely reliable copy of the original Hebrew Scriptures.

THE PRESERVATION OF THE NEW TESTAMENT

While the manuscript evidence for the Old Testament is encouraging, the manuscript evidence of the New Testament is unsurpassed by any other ancient book. There are more than 5,700 Greek manuscripts containing either parts or all of the New Testament text.[10] Compare this to Homer's *Iliad*, which only has 1,757 manuscripts in existence, or *Beowulf*, which comes to us from only one manuscript.

The wealth of manuscript evidence for the New Testament provides us with a tremendously accurate rendering of the original copies. While there are scribal variants in many of these manuscripts, most of the differences are insignificant errors such as misspellings and changes in word order.[11] Because we have so many manuscripts, biblical scholars are able to determine the wording of the original text in the vast majority of cases.[12]

FROM GOD TO YOU

While thousands of years have passed since God breathed out the Old and New Testament Scriptures, they remain the living, perfect Word of God today. Though the Scriptures have passed through countless scribes and many forms—from papyrus to paper to phone—you can be confident that the Word you read today is the very Word that was breathed out by God and written by the prophets and apostles.

HAS THE BIBLE REALLY BEEN PRESERVED FOR US TODAY?

When we examine the number and quality of manuscripts available, and the gap of time between the original and the earliest existing copies, there is overwhelming evidence that the text of the New Testament we have today is the same as the original.[13]

NUMBER OF KNOWN COPIES

33 TACITUS • ANNALS
WRITTEN – AD 100   EARLIEST MANUSCRIPT – AD 850

109 HERODOTUS • HISTORY
WRITTEN – 480 BC   EARLIEST MANUSCRIPT – AD 900

210 PLATO • TETRALOGIES
WRITTEN – 400 BC   EARLIEST MANUSCRIPT – AD 895

251 CAESAR • GALLIC WARS
WRITTEN – 100 BC   EARLIEST MANUSCRIPT – AD 800

1,757 HOMER • ILIAD
WRITTEN – 800 BC   EARLIEST MANUSCRIPT – 400 BC

NEW TESTAMENT
WRITTEN – AD 50–100   EARLIEST MANUSCRIPT – AD 130

1,000

3,000

5,000

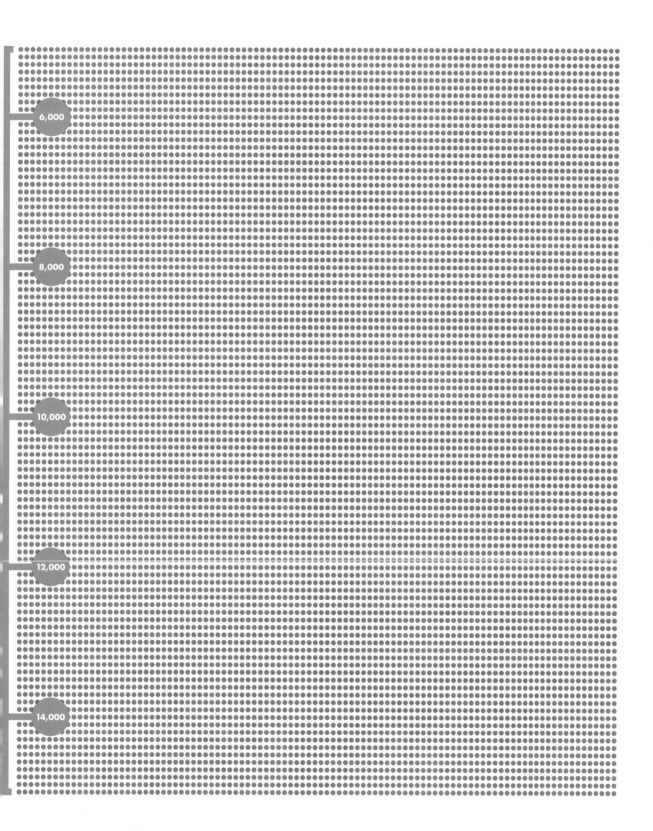

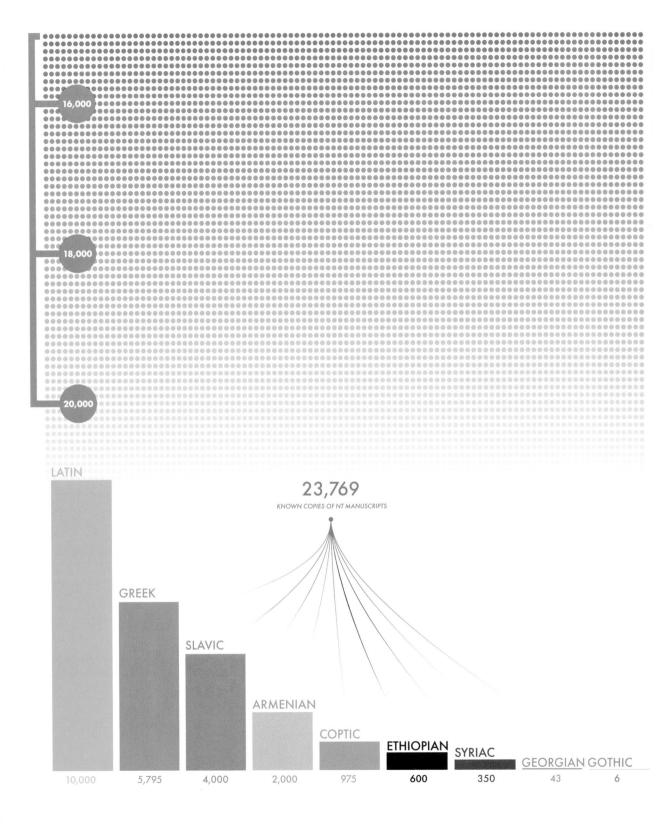

16,000

18,000

20,000

LATIN

GREEK

SLAVIC

ARMENIAN

COPTIC

ETHIOPIAN

SYRIAC

GEORGIAN GOTHIC

23,769
KNOWN COPIES OF NT MANUSCRIPTS

10,000   5,795   4,000   2,000   975   600   350   43   6

HOW WERE THE BOOKS COLLECTED?

In our digital age, we constantly receive updates and upgrades. By the time you read to the end of an online news article, it may have been revised and updated with new information. By the time you get around to buying the newest iPhone, a newer iPhone with brand-new technology is already hitting the market. With every update and upgrade, old information and old editions are rendered irrelevant.

So how do we know that the Bible, a book written thousands of years ago, won't undergo similar updates and upgrades in our day? How do we know that an undiscovered letter from Paul or an unknown gospel account isn't missing from the collection in our Bible? Besides that, how do we know that the books already contained within the Bible should be there? How can we be confident that the Bible we hold won't become irrelevant once a new edition comes out?

The Bible is a complete collection. Not a single word is missing, and not a single word can be added. Every book that should be in the Bible is already there, and we can be confident that there is no unknown book that will be added. The Bible will never be released in an updated and revised version. The Bible we hold is finished and final.

The books of the Bible are not a special class of man-made books handpicked by the church. Instead, the books of the Bible are God's written Word, which were recognized by the church as such. That's why it's not quite accurate to say that the books of the Bible were "chosen" or selected by a church council. More accurately, we should say they were "recognized." Over time, God's people recognized the books that were written by God and rejected the books that weren't.

The collection of writings that have been recognized are called "canon." F. F. Bruce defines the term in this way: "The Canon of Scripture . . . is the list of writings delivered to us as the divinely inspired record of God's self-revelation to men—that self-revelation of which Jesus Christ our Lord is the centre."[1] Although many factors affected why certain books made it into the canon, the primary question was whether God had written and inspired the book. If it wasn't from God, then it couldn't be a part of God's Word.

THE BOOKS OF THE BIBLE WERE RECOGNIZED FOR WHAT THEY ARE: GOD'S WRITTEN WORD

GE	EX	LV	NU	DT
JS	JU	RU	SA¹	SA²
KI¹	KI²	CH¹	CH²	EZ
NE	ES	JB	PS	PR
EC	SS	IS	JE	LA
EK	DA	HO	JO	AM
OB	JH	MI	NA	HA
ZP	HG	ZC	MA	

THE CANON OF THE OLD TESTAMENT

By the time Jesus began his ministry around AD 30, the canon of the Old Testament, known then as "the Hebrew Bible," was settled. In the four gospels, we find countless examples of Jesus debating with the teachers of the law and the Pharisees about what the Scripture means. But we never find Jesus debating with anyone about what the Scripture is. That's because by the time of Jesus, there was widespread agreement about the canon of the Old Testament. So, then, how did the canon of the Old Testament come about?

The canon began with God. God himself wrote the Ten Commandments on tablets of stone for Moses and the people of Israel: "The tablets were the work of God; the writing was the writing of God, engraved on the tablets" (Exodus 32:16). These tablets were stored and preserved in the ark of the covenant (Deuteronomy 10:5).[2]

The Ten Commandments formed the foundation for the "Book of the Law," or the Torah, which were the five books that Moses wrote: Genesis, Exodus, Leviticus, Numbers, and Deuteronomy.

Moses's successor, Joshua, continued the practice of writing down words "in the Book of the Law of God" (Joshua 24:26). After Joshua, a succession of other men of God, most of whom were prophets, recorded the words of God, telling of God's great acts and his covenant promises to his people. The people of God always believed that these holy writings were God's words, just as God had told the prophet Jeremiah: "This is what the LORD, the God of Israel, says: 'Write in a book all the words I have spoken to you'" (Jeremiah 30:2).

With each divinely authorized prophet, the canon of the Old Testament grew, until the last of the Old Testament prophets, Malachi, wrote around 475 BC.[3] This was probably around the time that Nehemiah finished his work too. This means that since 475 BC, nearly twenty-five hundred years ago, the books within the Old Testament canon have remained the same.

By one account, there are 682 claims to divine authority in the Torah, 1,307 claims in the prophetic books, 418 claims in the historical books, and 195 claims in the poetic books.[4] This means that the Old Testament Scriptures were written with the understanding that they were God's holy Word, and they have always been understood in this way.[5]

DATES OT BOOKS WERE WRITTEN

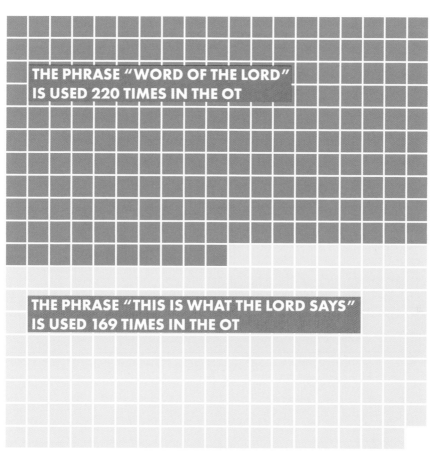

THE PHRASE "WORD OF THE LORD" IS USED 220 TIMES IN THE OT

THE PHRASE "THIS IS WHAT THE LORD SAYS" IS USED 169 TIMES IN THE OT

THESE ARE ONLY TWO PHRASES OF MANY THAT EXPRESS DIVINE AUTHORITY IN THE SCRIPTURES

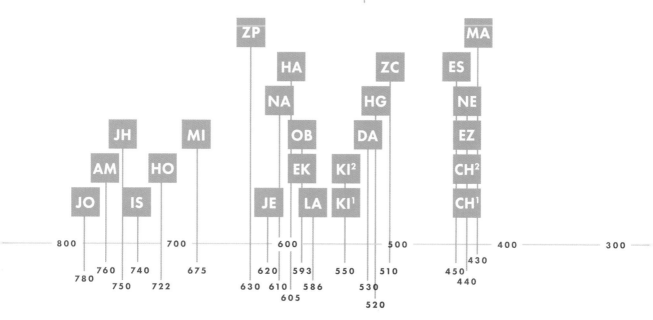

THE CANON OF THE
NEW TESTAMENT

Before Jesus' death and resurrection, he promised to empower his disciples to remember all that he taught them so they could teach others: "But when he, the Spirit of truth, comes, he will guide you into all the truth. He will not speak on his own; he will speak only what he hears, and he will tell you what is yet to come" (John 16:13).

The writings of the disciples show that they understood their work to be the fulfillment of Jesus' promise. They were speaking God's words with God's authority. For example, the apostle Paul tells the church in Corinth, "What I am writing to you is the Lord's command" (1 Corinthians 14:37). Even the apostle Peter called Paul's writings *graphē*, a term referring to holy Scripture when it is used in the New Testament (2 Peter 3:16).

Jesus' promise to guide the apostles' teaching provided the foundational litmus test for the New Testament canon: works written by or authorized by an apostle were accepted. For this reason, Matthew's gospel, John's gospel, Paul's

letters, James's letter, Peter's letters, John's letters, and John's Revelation were eventually accepted into the canon, since they were all known to be written by disciples. Mark's gospel was accepted because of his association with Peter, and Luke's gospel and the book of Acts were accepted because of his association with Paul. Jude was accepted because of his association with James—not to mention his status as the half brother of Jesus.

The book of Hebrews, whose author is unknown, is the exception to the rule. While many in the early church believed that Paul was responsible for the letter, the mystery has never been resolved. Why, then, is the letter still included in the canon? Because from the early church until today, all Christians who read Hebrews can testify to its divine origin. The inclusion of Hebrews in the canon demonstrates the second criterion for inclusion: there needed to be a general consensus or recognition by the church that the book was God's Word. If it was not in widespread use across the churches,

> *Through the first few centuries of church history, councils, churches, and leaders would put forth different collections of writings to be recognized for inclusion in the canon. What follows are several major collections that helped shape the New Testament.*[6]

AD 170
THE MURATORIAN CANON

 RECOGNIZED AS CANONICAL

SPURIOUS & REJECTED WRITINGS
PAUL TO THE LAODICEANS
PAUL TO THE ALEXANDRIANS
SHEPHERD OF HERMAS
(AND OTHER GNOSTIC WRITINGS)

MT MATTHEW **MK** MARK **LK** LUKE **JN** JOHN

MID–THIRD CENTURY
ORIGEN'S CANON

 AC ACTS

 RO ROMANS   **CO¹** 1 CORINTHIANS   **CO²** 2 CORINTHIANS   **GA** GALATIANS   **EP** EPHESIANS   **PH** PHILIPPIANS

 CS COLOSSIANS   **TH¹** 1 THESSALONIANS   **TH²** 2 THESSALONIANS   **TI¹** 1 TIMOTHY   **TI²** 2 TIMOTHY   **TT** TITUS   **PL** PHILEMON

 HE HEBREWS   **JA** JAMES   **PE¹** 1 PETER   **PE²** 2 PETER   **JN¹** 1 JOHN   **JN²** 2 JOHN   **JN³** 3 JOHN   **JU** JUDE

RECOGNIZED AS CANONICAL

NOT YET RECOGNIZED

RE REVELATION

MT MATTHEW **MK** MARK **LK** LUKE **JN** JOHN

 AC ACTS

MID–FOURTH CENTURY
EUSEBIUS'S CANON

 RO ROMANS **CO¹** 1 CORINTHIANS **CO²** 2 CORINTHIANS **GA** GALATIANS **EP** EPHESIANS **PH** PHILIPPIANS

 CS COLOSSIANS **TH¹** 1 THESSALONIANS **TH²** 2 THESSALONIANS **TI¹** 1 TIMOTHY **TI²** 2 TIMOTHY **TT** TITUS **PL** PHILEMON

 HE HEBREWS **JA** JAMES **PE¹** 1 PETER **PE²** 2 PETER **JN¹** 1 JOHN **JN²** 2 JOHN **JN³** 3 JOHN **JU** JUDE

 RE REVELATION **RECOGNIZED AS CANONICAL**
NOT YET RECOGNIZED

SPURIOUS & REJECTED WRITINGS
ACTS OF PAUL
SHEPHERD OF HERMAS
DIDACHE
LETTER OF BARNABAS
REVELATION OF PETER
GOSPEL ACCORDING TO THE HEBREWS
GOSPEL OF PETER
GOSPEL OF THOMAS
GOSPEL OF MATTHIAS
ACTS OF ANDREW
ACTS OF JOHN
ACTS OF OTHERS

it could not be recognized as Scripture. Acknowledging the mystery behind the authorship of Hebrews, Jerome wrote in AD 414, "It does not matter whose it is, since it is the work of a churchman . . . and honored daily by being read in the churches."[7] Although the authorship of the letter is still debatable, Christian readers will find it difficult to deny that God was ultimately behind its writing.

Besides being authored or authorized by an apostle and receiving general recognition from the church, the book also could not disagree with other Scriptures. Because God never lies or contradicts himself, God's Word cannot contradict itself.

While the writing of the New Testament canon was most likely complete around AD 94–96, the canon of the New Testament took longer. It was officially recognized in the mid-fourth century at the latest. Athanasius's "Festal Letter" in AD 367 contained the same twenty-seven books that are in our New Testament today.[8]

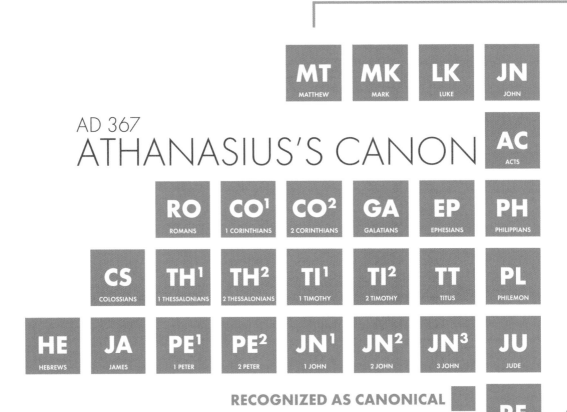

AD 367
ATHANASIUS'S CANON

MT MATTHEW · MK MARK · LK LUKE · JN JOHN · AC ACTS
RO ROMANS · CO¹ 1 CORINTHIANS · CO² 2 CORINTHIANS · GA GALATIANS · EP EPHESIANS · PH PHILIPPIANS
CS COLOSSIANS · TH¹ 1 THESSALONIANS · TH² 2 THESSALONIANS · TI¹ 1 TIMOTHY · TI² 2 TIMOTHY · TT TITUS · PL PHILEMON
HE HEBREWS · JA JAMES · PE¹ 1 PETER · PE² 2 PETER · JN¹ 1 JOHN · JN² 2 JOHN · JN³ 3 JOHN · JU JUDE

RECOGNIZED AS CANONICAL

RE REVELATION

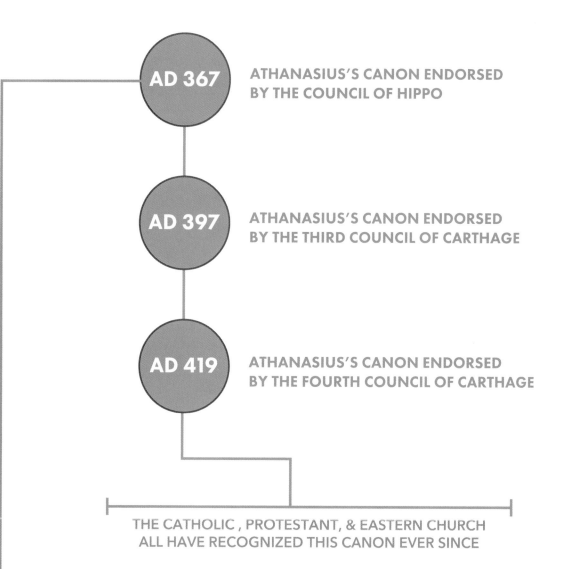

AD 367 — ATHANASIUS'S CANON ENDORSED BY THE COUNCIL OF HIPPO

AD 397 — ATHANASIUS'S CANON ENDORSED BY THE THIRD COUNCIL OF CARTHAGE

AD 419 — ATHANASIUS'S CANON ENDORSED BY THE FOURTH COUNCIL OF CARTHAGE

THE CATHOLIC , PROTESTANT, & EASTERN CHURCH
ALL HAVE RECOGNIZED THIS CANON EVER SINCE

All of the books in both the Old and New Testament are time-tested, doctrinally sound, and divinely inspired. We can be sure that all of the books in the Bible belong. But how do we know that there aren't more books that need to be added?

CAN ANY BOOKS BE ADDED?

If God spoke through Israel's prophets and Jesus' disciples, why can't he continue to speak in this way today? What is keeping him from raising up a new prophet or a new disciple to write another letter or another gospel account?

Books like the Quran and the Book of Mormon are attempts to add new revelation to the canon. Those who consider these books as revelation suggest that the Old and New Testaments were just one of many phases of God's revelation.

But the Bible itself has something different to say about how God has chosen to speak to us. Hebrews 1:1–2 reads, "In the past God spoke to our ancestors through the prophets at many times and in various ways, but in these last days he has spoken to us by his Son, whom he appointed heir of all things." The author divides God's spoken revelation into two eras: "in the past" and "in these last days," which is the era spanning from Jesus' ascension to Jesus' second coming. Once, God spoke through his prophets, but now, in the last days, he speaks by the Son.

The revelation of the Son through the New Testament Scriptures is God's final and sufficient Word to us until the Son comes again. Until that day when we see God face-to-face, there is no more Scripture to be added. John Frame writes, "For God to add more books to the canon would be like his adding something to the work of Christ, something Scripture teaches cannot be done. So, the canon is closed today, not only in the sense that human beings dare not add to it, but also in the sense that God himself will not add to it."[9]

We can trust that God has faithfully handed down to us the books and letters that he wanted to be included in the canon. The Bible is a collection without need for revision, since every book is authorized and breathed out by God. And the Bible is a collection without need for addition, since the Word given to us by Jesus is all we need until he comes again.

WHAT ABOUT THOSE OTHER BOOKS?

GE	EX	LV	NU	DT
JS	JU	RU	SA¹	SA²
KI¹	KI²	CH¹	CH²	EZ
NE	ES	JB	PS	PR
EC	SS	IS	JE	LA
EK	DA	HO	JO	AM
OB	JH	MI	NA	HA
ZP	HG	ZC	MA	

✚

SI	WS	MC¹	MC²	TO
BD	JU	ES²	BA	

If you flip open a Roman Catholic Bible, you may notice several extra books that aren't included in the Protestant canon. These are called the "Apocrypha," and they were written during the period between Malachi and the coming of Christ (approximately 475 BC–AD 30). They include books like Tobit, Judith, Sirach, and 1 and 2 Maccabees.

While there was some debate in the early church over whether the Apocrypha should be included in the canon, the Jewish people never accepted these books as Scripture. For example, Jesus and his disciples quote the Old Testament Scriptures as divinely authoritative almost three hundred times, but they never quote the Apocrypha as divinely authoritative.[10]

While Jerome added the Apocrypha to the Latin Vulgate, he made it clear that they were "books of the church" and not to be treated as equal to the Scriptures.[11] The Roman Catholic Church, however, increasingly relied on the Apocrypha until the Council of Trent in 1546, when they officially declared the Apocrypha to be a part of the canon. The Reformers, in contrast, returned to the traditional view of the Apocrypha as helpful for the church but not a part of the canon.

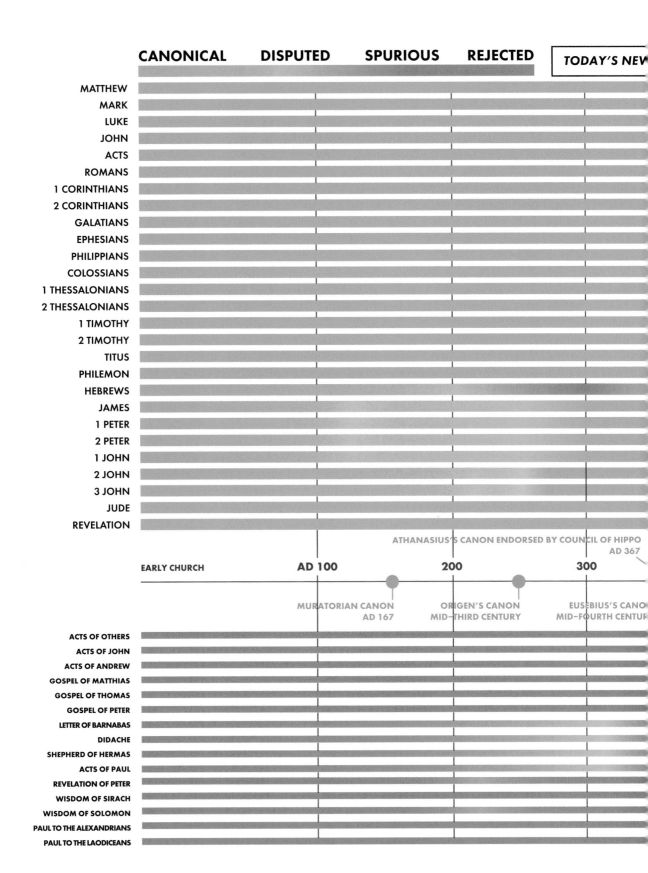

CANONICAL   DISPUTED   SPURIOUS   REJECTED   TODAY'S NEW

MATTHEW
MARK
LUKE
JOHN
ACTS
ROMANS
1 CORINTHIANS
2 CORINTHIANS
GALATIANS
EPHESIANS
PHILIPPIANS
COLOSSIANS
1 THESSALONIANS
2 THESSALONIANS
1 TIMOTHY
2 TIMOTHY
TITUS
PHILEMON
HEBREWS
JAMES
1 PETER
2 PETER
1 JOHN
2 JOHN
3 JOHN
JUDE
REVELATION

ATHANASIUS'S CANON ENDORSED BY COUNCIL OF HIPPO
AD 367

EARLY CHURCH   AD 100   200   300

MURATORIAN CANON   ORIGEN'S CANON   EUSEBIUS'S CANON
AD 167   MID–THIRD CENTURY   MID–FOURTH CENTUR

ACTS OF OTHERS
ACTS OF JOHN
ACTS OF ANDREW
GOSPEL OF MATTHIAS
GOSPEL OF THOMAS
GOSPEL OF PETER
LETTER OF BARNABAS
DIDACHE
SHEPHERD OF HERMAS
ACTS OF PAUL
REVELATION OF PETER
WISDOM OF SIRACH
WISDOM OF SOLOMON
PAUL TO THE ALEXANDRIANS
PAUL TO THE LAODICEANS

ATHANASIUS'S CANON ENDORSED BY THIRD COUNCIL OF CARTHAGE
AD 397

400   **500**   **600**   **700**   **800**

ATHANASIUS'S CANON ENDORSED BY FOURTH COUNCIL OF CARTHAGE
AD 419

CHAPTER FOUR

WHAT MAKES THE BIBLE UNIQUE?

As the Preacher wrote Ecclesiastes, he lamented over the unending publishing of the written word: "Of making many books there is no end" (Ecclesiastes 12:12). But not even Solomon in all of his wisdom could have anticipated the flurry of content being published today. Had he known of the digital revolution and the rise of mass media, he might have added, "Of making many books and movies and television shows and blogs and podcasts there is no end."

Never before in the history of the world have we had so many voices begging for our ears. It's not as if people have changed. In all times and in all places, people have had their own opinions. But never before has everyone been given so many outlets to share their opinion.

Out of the midst of millions of human voices, the Bible stands apart. While these voices give advice on how to order our lives, the Bible alone is sufficient. While these voices contradict one another and offer questionable counsel, the Bible is crystal clear about our Creator and his design for the creation. While these voices claim to be truth, the Bible alone holds the supreme seat as the ultimate truth of God. We desperately need the Bible in order to live.

The Bible is unique, set apart from every other book written and every other voice spoken. Theologians have organized the distinct characteristics of the Bible into four categories. We can remember these with the acronym "SCAN": the sufficiency, clarity, authority, and necessity of Scripture.[1] These four qualities set the Bible apart from everything else.

(1)

THE BIBLE IS SUFFCIENT
IT INCLUDES EVERYTHING WE NEED FOR
SALVATION —— FAITH —— OBEDIENCE

TI²
3:15-17
ESV

> You have been acquainted with the sacred writings, which are able to make you wise for salvation through faith in Christ Jesus. All Scripture is breathed out by God and profitable for teaching, for reproof, for correction, and for training in righteousness, that the man of God may be complete, equipped for every good work.

THE SCRIPTURES
MAKE US WISE
MAKE US COMPLETE
TO
FULLY OBEY GOD

The sufficiency of the Bible means that the Bible contains all we need for salvation and for the Christian life. Paul makes this attribute of Scripture clear in his second letter to Timothy: "From infancy you have known the Holy Scriptures, which are able to make you wise for salvation through faith in Christ Jesus. All Scripture is God-breathed and is useful for teaching, rebuking, correcting and training in righteousness, so that the servant of God may be thoroughly equipped for every good work" (3:15–17). The Scriptures are able to make someone wise for salvation, and the Scriptures make us fully equipped to obey God.

The sufficiency of Scripture does not mean we should do away with Bible teachers, Christian books, and group Bible studies in the Christian life. These are some of the best ways we can grow. But the sufficiency of Scripture does mean we should aim to listen to preaching, read books, and join Bible studies that are most saturated with the Scriptures, since the Scriptures have all we need for the Christian life.

Of course, the Bible isn't sufficient to teach us about everything. The Bible, for example, won't tell you how to bake a cake or train for a marathon. But the Bible will tell you all you need for knowing and obeying God.

Because the Bible is sufficient, we are forbidden to add or take away from it. We are not to declare anything sinful that God does not declare or imply to be sinful in his Word, and we are not to require anything that God does not require of us in his Word.[2] This was the sin of the Pharisees, who were adding to Scripture by "teaching as doctrines the commandments of men" (Matthew 15:9 ESV) and taking away from Scripture by neglecting "justice and the love of God" (Luke 11:42).

The sufficiency of Scripture should make us pause and worship God for his provision. When we hold the Bible, we hold the full counsel of God for us as his children. We don't have to wonder about who God is or what God expects of us. He gives us all we need in his written Word.

(2)

THE BIBLE IS CLEAR

IT CAN BE UNDERSTOOD BY ALL WHO READ WITH

DEPENDENCE ON GOD

SUBMISSION TO GOD'S WILL

The clarity of the Bible means that the Bible "ensures its meaning is accessible to all who come to it in faith."[3] In other words, the Bible is not a collection of obscure wisdom meant to confuse us. It is given by God for us to read, receive, and respond.

Many unbelievers who first approach the Bible will claim that the Bible doesn't make any sense or that its language doesn't fit today's culture. While there are certainly passages of Scripture that require deep thought and consideration, to claim that God's Word is unclear is an offense against God's character. If the Scriptures are God's Word (and they are), then those who call the Scriptures unclear are calling God unclear.

But "God is not a God of confusion" (1 Corinthians 14:33 ESV). God wrote his Word in such a way that any person, regardless of culture or education level, would be able to understand it. As the psalmist wrote, "The statutes of the LORD are trustworthy, making wise the simple" (Psalm 19:7). God's Word is trustworthy and sure, not unclear. It makes wise not only the educated but also the uneducated.

This is how the Bible describes itself. Psalm 119:105 says that the Scriptures are clarifying light, not confusing darkness: "Your word is a lamp for my feet, a light on my path." Psalm 19:7 says that the Scriptures provide wisdom not just for the wise but also for the simple. Deuteronomy 30:11–14 says that the Scriptures are not difficult enough so that we are freed from the requirement of obedience, but they are clear enough so that we are expected to obey.

The clarity of Scripture is not the same as the easiness of Scriptures. The Scriptures are clear, but they are sometimes "hard to understand," as Peter says of Paul's writings (2 Peter 3:16). God expects us to sow effort, prayer, and thought into the study of Scripture so that with the Spirit's help, we can reap the reward of understanding.

To understand the Scriptures, we must have the Spirit of God and the "mind of Christ" (1 Corinthians 2:15–16). Those who approach the Scriptures with stubbornness and pride will find them hard to understand. But those who approach the Scriptures with dependence on God and a desire to obey him will discover the glorious clarity of the Word. The clarity of Scripture is experienced most by those who approach it as the psalmist did: "Be good to your servant while I live, that I may obey your word. Open my eyes that I may see wonderful things in your law" (Psalm 119:17–18).

THE BIBLE IS AUTHORITATIVE

IT IS GOD'S WORD WITH GOD'S AUTHORITY

DISBELIEF AND DISOBEDIENCE TO SCRIPTURE **=** DISBELIEF AND DISOBEDIENCE TO GOD

The authority of the Bible means that the Bible's Word is God's Word with God's authority, so that "to disbelieve or disobey any word of Scripture is to disbelieve or disobey God."[4] The Bible is the Supreme Court of all truth, and all other lesser authorities must align with it or be rejected. The Bible is God's Word in such a way that how we respond to the Bible is how we respond to God.

The Hebrew Scriptures were always considered to be the authoritative words of God. The 415 occurrences of "Thus says the LORD" within the Old Testament show that it was written and understood as the very words of God that carried God's authority. The apostles understood themselves as the successors of Israel's prophets writing the words of God, as Peter shows: "I want you to recall the words spoken in the past by the holy prophets and the command given by our Lord and Savior through your apostles" (2 Peter 3:2). From the first words in Genesis to the last words in Revelation, the Bible is the authoritative Word of God.

This doesn't mean we are forbidden from using and appealing to lesser authorities, such as scholars, our observations, or our emotions. These all have their place.

HOWEVER, THE AUTHORITY OF SCRIPTURE
DOES MEAN THAT
IF ANY LESSER
AUTHORITY CONTRADICTS
THE BIBLE
LIKE

SCHOLARS | OUR OBSERVATIONS | OUR EMOTIONS

THE BIBLE WINS THE DAY

THE BIBLE IS NECESSARY

FOR SALVATION & SPIRITUAL LIFE

To say that the Bible is necessary means that the Bible is required for salvation and spiritual life. To be sure, we don't need the Bible to know that God exists. The psalmist asserts, "The heavens declare the glory of God; the skies proclaim the work of his hands" (Psalm 19:1). And Paul writes, "What may be known about God is plain to [humanity], because God has made it plain to them. For since the creation of the world God's invisible qualities—his eternal power and divine nature—have been clearly seen, being understood from what has been made" (Romans 1:19–20).

WE DON'T NEED THE BIBLE TO KNOW THAT GOD EXISTS

BUT WE DO NEED THE BIBLE TO KNOW GOD

By this, we mean that the Word of God is required to have a saving knowledge of God. This is what Paul lays out in Romans 10:17: "Faith comes from hearing the message, and the message is heard through the word about Christ." Peter affirms that we are born again "through the living and enduring word of God" (1 Peter 1:23). While we can know something about God from creation, we can only know the fullness of God's plan of salvation in Christ through his Word.

The Bible is not only necessary for our salvation, but also for our spiritual life. Jesus reiterated this truth as he quoted Deuteronomy in the desert: "It is written: 'Man shall not live on bread alone, but on every word that comes from the mouth of God'" (Matthew 4:4). Just as we need food and drink to sustain us physically, we need the Bible to sustain us spiritually. And just as the neglect of food and drink will deprive and harm us physically, neglecting the Bible will do the same to us spiritually.

Just as the sufficiency of Scripture tells us that God has given us everything we need for life and godliness in the Scriptures, the necessity of Scripture tells us that we cannot have life and godliness apart from the Scriptures. To grow up into the knowledge and likeness of God, we must take in the Scriptures as readily and frequently as newborn infants take milk (1 Peter 2:2–3).

A BOOK ON ITS OWN

There are thousands of classic Christian books that deserve to be read by every believer. We have relied on some excellent books in preparing this one. But the truth is that you could endure without all of them—and without this one as well. Only the Bible is sufficient, giving you all you need for life and godliness. Only the Bible imparts knowledge about the Godhead in a way that the simplest person could understand. Only the Bible stands above all other authorities. Only the Bible is necessary to be saved and grow spiritually.

The Bible stands on its own as the one book you cannot do without. This is why our great hope for this book is that it drives you to that book!

CHAPTER FIVE

CAN WE TRUST THE BIBLE?

- HISTORICALLY
- SCIENTIFICALLY
- CULTURALLY
- SPIRITUALLY

Since the dawn of the Enlightenment in the late seventeenth century, when reason was elevated as the highest authority, people have been increasingly reluctant to accept the Bible's claims to authority. Whereas the Bible once inspected our lives and revealed our sin, now we have begun to inspect the pages of the Bible in an attempt to reveal its errors. Over time, doubts began to arise about the trustworthiness of the Bible and its ability to speak with authority. Many today claim that the Bible is outdated, irrelevant, and even offensive.

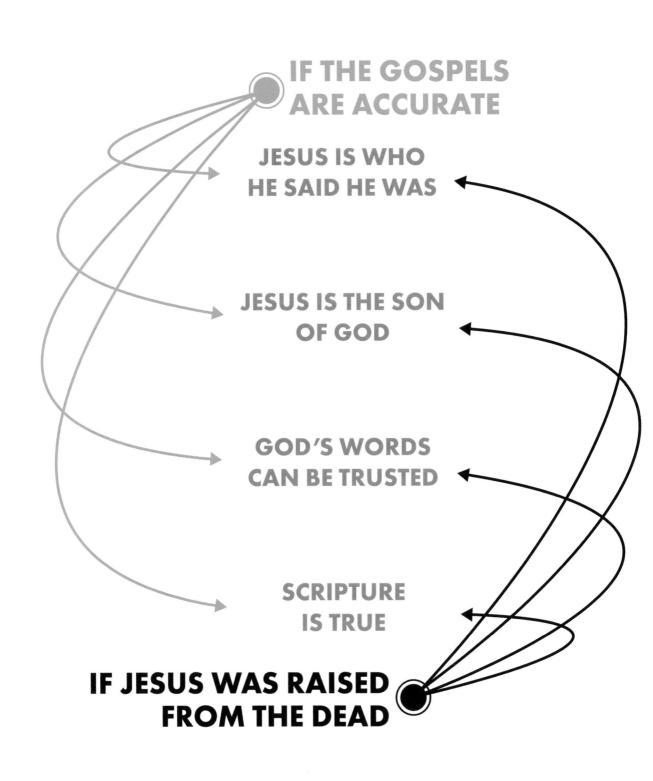

IF THE GOSPELS
ARE ACCURATE

JESUS IS WHO
HE SAID HE WAS

JESUS IS THE SON
OF GOD

GOD'S WORDS
CAN BE TRUSTED

SCRIPTURE
IS TRUE

IF JESUS WAS RAISED
FROM THE DEAD

WE CAN TRUST THE BIBLE HISTORICALLY

In his bestselling book *The Reason for God*, Timothy Keller explains how the Bible can be trusted, even amid historical, scientific, and cultural challenges.[1] Keller highlights that the most significant question about the historicity of the Bible is whether the gospel accounts—Matthew, Mark, Luke, and John—are historically reliable. If the gospels accurately report who Jesus was and what he said and did, then Jesus really did raise from the dead and Jesus really is the Son of God. And if Jesus is the Son of God, then all of his words can be trusted—including his belief that all of Scripture was God's true and reliable Word. Jesus said that the Scriptures could not be set aside (John 10:35), that they were the Word of God (Matthew 15:6; Mark 7:13), and that he was the fulfillment of all the Scriptures (Matthew 5:17).

When the Bible began to be tested under the lens of historical criticism, many believed that the gospel accounts were nothing more than invented legends about a man named Jesus, a noble Jewish teacher. But today's manuscript evidence shows that it is likely that the gospel accounts were written within forty to sixty years after Jesus' death.[2] The gospel writers also included details in their accounts that could have been verified or denied by those who were still alive during Jesus' ministry, crucifixion, and resurrection. If, for example, Jesus had not been raised from the dead, there would have been many alive who witnessed Jesus' death and burial who could have refuted the gospels' claims. But the gospel writers knew that no one could refute the resurrection, and so they wrote and published their accounts and boldly preached that Jesus had been raised from the dead.

In addition, the gospels demonstrate all of the characteristics of reliable history rather than a legend written to support a growing church movement. In the gospels, the disciples—who would eventually become the church's leaders—are shown quarreling with one another, misunderstanding Jesus, and abandoning Jesus during his arrest. If the church wanted to make up a story about their religious leader, would they have written that he was crucified alone while his closest followers abandoned him? The most likely reason the authors of the gospel accounts recorded this fact is that it was true.[3]

ARE THE GOSPELS WE HAVE TODAY
ACCURATE & RELIABLE?

OBJECTION #1

THE GOSPELS WERE WRITTEN AFTER THE FIRST CENTURY

1ST-CENTURY NAMES ARE ACCURATE

The most popular names found in the gospels are the most popular names found in Palestine in the first century.
If the writers were simply guessing about the names they were using in their accounts, they happened to guess with remarkable accuracy.

1ST-CENTURY LANGUAGE IS ACCURATE

The gospel writers appear to have written in a style that was similar to those who lived at that time.

1ST-CENTURY LOCATIONS ARE ACCURATE

The gospel writers didn't just write about big locations like Jerusalem like many late writers did, but about smaller villages and landmarks only a first-century resident would have been familiar with.

IF WRITTEN LATER, THERE ARE ODD OMISSIONS

The NT predicts the destruction of the temple but doesn't describe or verify the event.
If the writers were there during this event or after it, they would have included a description.

The NT doesn't describe the siege of Jerusalem, even though it would support the theme of suffering.

Luke does mention the death of prominent Christian leaders like Stephen and James but doesn't mention the deaths of Paul or Peter.

If the gospels are late fabrications, Mark & Luke are not ideal choices as authors, since they were not eyewitnesses.

ARCHAEOLOGY HAS CONFIRMED MANY NAMES & LOCATIONS ONCE THOUGHT TO BE INACCURATE

THE GOSPELS ARE ACCURATE

Quirinius - governor of Syria
Pontius Pilate
Lysanias
City of Iconium located in Phrygia
Pool of Siloam
Pool of Bethesda

NEW IDEAS WERE INVENTED THROUGH THE CENTURIES

THERE IS A CONSISTENT PRESERVATION OF THEME AND CONTENT FROM THE STUDENTS OF JOHN, PAUL, AND PETER.

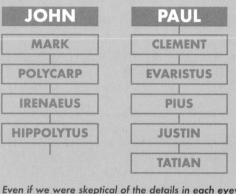

JOHN	PAUL	PETER
MARK	CLEMENT	MARK
POLYCARP	EVARISTUS	JUSTUS
IRENAEUS	PIUS	PANTAENUS
HIPPOLYTUS	JUSTIN	CLEMENT
	TATIAN	ORIGEN
		PAMPHILUS
		EUSEBIUS

AD 50–100

AD 350

Even if we were skeptical of the details in each eyewitness account, there is no doubt about the major themes and claims of the gospels. Jesus was described as God, claimed to be God, walked with his disciples, taught many people, died on a cross, and rose from the dead. This version of Jesus is not a late invention or exaggeration. This version of Jesus was witnessed and accurately described by the gospel writers and confirmed by their students.[4]

L J

THE GOSPELS ARE RELIABLE

THE TEXT HAS CHANGED THROUGH THE CENTURIES

THE QUALITY & QUANTITY OF MANUSCRIPTS AVAILABLE & THE SHORT SPAN OF TIME FROM ORIGINAL TO OUR EARLIEST COPIES MAKE THIS CLAIM EXTREMELY UNLIKELY.

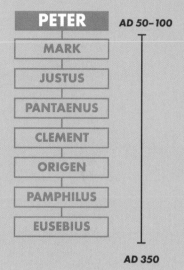

EARLIEST MANUSCRIPT – AD 130

WRITTEN – AD 50–100

MORE THAN 20,000 COPIES OF NT MANUSCRIPTS EXIST

BEFORE COMPUTERS, COPY MACHINES, AND THE CLOUD, IMPORTANT RECORDS, DOCUMENTS, AND BOOKS ALL HAD TO BE COPIED BY HAND. THE PROFESSIONAL SCRIBE WAS A HIGH POSITION IN SOCIETY, AND DUE TO THE NATURE OF THEIR WORK, THEY WERE METICULOUS IN THEIR PREPARATION AND PRACTICE.[5]

IS THE OLD TESTAMENT WE HAVE TODAY ACCURATE?

1 The manuscript must be written on the skins of clean animals.

2 It must be fastened together with strings of clean animals.

THROUGHOUT HISTORY, MANY SCRIBES USED DIFFERENT METHODS TO ENSURE THAT THEY WERE COPYING AS PRECISELY AS POSSIBLE. WHILE SOME PRACTICES AND RITUALS HAVE BEEN EMBELLISHED, UNDOUBTEDLY THERE WERE SOME THAT PRACTICED ANY NUMBER OR VERSION OF THESE METHODS. THE DATE OF THESE PRESCRIPTIONS IS UNKNOWN, BUT ITS ROOTS DATE TO THE BABYLONIAN TALMUD.

13 Three lines of space must be between each book.

A space the width of nine consonants must come between each section.

12 No word may touch another word.

11

14 The book of Deuteronomy must end with a line.

15 The scribe must wash his entire body before beginning to copy.

16 Every time the name of God is written, the pen must be wiped clean and have fresh ink.

17 Before the name of God YHWH was written, the scribe would wash his entire body.

18 When finished, the scribe would find the middle word and compare it to the middle word of the original.

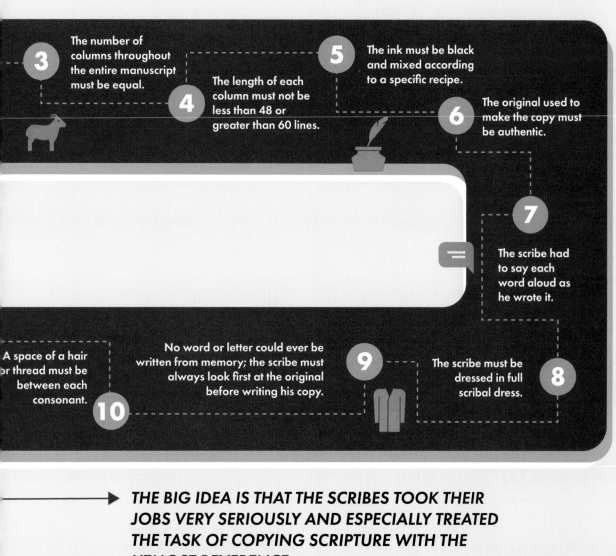

3 The number of columns throughout the entire manuscript must be equal.

4 The length of each column must not be less than 48 or greater than 60 lines.

5 The ink must be black and mixed according to a specific recipe.

6 The original used to make the copy must be authentic.

7 The scribe had to say each word aloud as he wrote it.

8 The scribe must be dressed in full scribal dress.

9 No word or letter could ever be written from memory; the scribe must always look first at the original before writing his copy.

10 A space of a hair or thread must be between each consonant.

THE BIG IDEA IS THAT THE SCRIBES TOOK THEIR JOBS VERY SERIOUSLY AND ESPECIALLY TREATED THE TASK OF COPYING SCRIPTURE WITH THE UTMOST REVERENCE.

19 When finished, the scribe would find the middle letter and compare it to the middle letter of the original.

20 If a sheet had one mistake, the entire sheet was thrown out. If a sheet was found to have three mistakes, the entire manuscript was thrown out.

21 Statistics counting each word and letter were kept. If the counts did not match from the copy to the original, the entire manuscript was thrown out.

HAS HISTORY PROVED THE BIBLE TO BE TEXTUALLY RELIABLE?

OT

DEAD SEA SCROLLS
200 BC–AD 70

EN-GEDI SCROLL
3RD–4TH CENTURY AD

The variants in both are obvious errors, spelling changes, and conjunction additions.

MASORETIC TEXT
AD 1000

95% THE SAME

99.9% THE SAME

For centuries, the oldest available copy of an OT manuscript was the Masoretic Text, which was copied around the year AD 1000. In 1946 and 1970, portions of OT manuscripts were discovered that predated the Masoretic Text by 1,000 years. When they were compared, scholars realized that over this time span, the Old Testament text has remained virtually unchanged.

NT

There are approximately 20,000 lines of text in the New Testament. Because there are so many ancient NT manuscripts to compare, only .2% are in doubt of being accurate to the original text.

None of these variants affect major beliefs or doctrines in any way.

THE SCIENCE OF
TEXTUAL CRITICISM
SUGGESTS THE BIBLE
WE HAVE IS A
RELIABLE AND
ACCURATE
TRANSLATION OF THE
ORIGINAL
AUTOGRAPHS

THE BELIEVER IS PROVIDED FURTHER ASSURANCE

EVIDENCE OF APOLOGETICS & PHILOSOPHY

PROVIDENCE OF GOD

WITNESS OF THE HOLY SPIRIT

WE CAN TRUST THAT
OUR BIBLE TODAY
IS THE SAME BIBLE
THAT GOD
INSTRUCTED THE
PROPHETS AND
APOSTLES TO WRITE

WE CAN TRUST THE BIBLE SCIENTIFICALLY

Those who reject the Bible often do so because it appears to contradict scientific findings. The Bible says that God created the heavens and the earth in seven days and that we all came from one man and one woman, Adam and Eve. But some argue that science has proven that the earth is billions of years old and that we have evolved from a different species.

While science and the Bible are often pitted against one another, the truth is that if God breathed out the Bible and created the world, there is no inherent conflict between the two. Apologist Frank Turek writes, "God and science are not competing explanations for the universe and life, any more than Henry Ford and the laws of internal combustion are competing explanations for the Model T. Both are necessary. Learning more about how a car works will never disprove the existence of the carmaker."[6]

Our approach to apparent conflicts between the Bible and science depends on our worldview. Those with a naturalistic worldview will rule out from the beginning any notion of God's intervention in the world. But those who approach the question with a Christian worldview acknowledge that science works only because God intervenes in the world. Without God holding all things together, natural laws could not be depended on. As Albert Einstein commented, "The eternal mystery of the world is its comprehensibility . . . The fact that it is comprehensible is a miracle."[7]

If we approach the Scriptures with a theistic worldview, then the miracles described in the Bible are not a stumbling block. While miracles do disrupt the normal flow of nature, if there is a God, then it is not surprising that he can work miraculously in creation. Keller writes, "If there is a Creator God, there is nothing illogical at all about the possibility of miracles. After all, if he created everything out of nothing, it would hardly be a problem for him to rearrange parts of it as and when he wishes."[8]

Likewise, if you believe in God, then it is only logical that he created the heavens and the earth, including mankind, as Genesis states. Believing in a Creator God does rule out the possibility of evolution as a worldview, that all of creation came about simply as the result of natural processes. But believing in a Creator God does not contradict science, since science cannot disprove the existence of God.[9] While the Bible tells us who created the world and is incompatible with a macroevolutionary worldview, it does leave the door open for science to explain much of how the world has developed from creation into the present day.

DOES MY WORLDVIEW REALLY MATTER?

YOUR CREATION WORLDVIEW AFFECTS HOW YOU ANSWER LIFE'S BIGGEST QUESTIONS

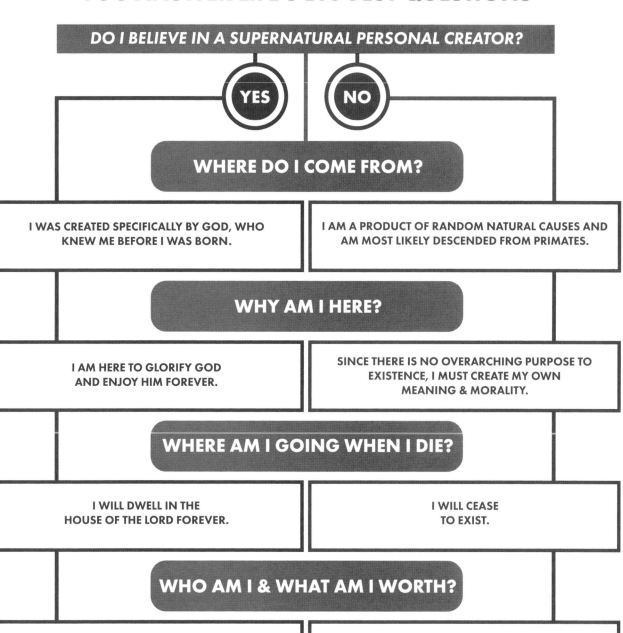

DO I BELIEVE IN A SUPERNATURAL PERSONAL CREATOR?

YES   NO

WHERE DO I COME FROM?

I WAS CREATED SPECIFICALLY BY GOD, WHO KNEW ME BEFORE I WAS BORN.

I AM A PRODUCT OF RANDOM NATURAL CAUSES AND AM MOST LIKELY DESCENDED FROM PRIMATES.

WHY AM I HERE?

I AM HERE TO GLORIFY GOD AND ENJOY HIM FOREVER.

SINCE THERE IS NO OVERARCHING PURPOSE TO EXISTENCE, I MUST CREATE MY OWN MEANING & MORALITY.

WHERE AM I GOING WHEN I DIE?

I WILL DWELL IN THE HOUSE OF THE LORD FOREVER.

I WILL CEASE TO EXIST.

WHO AM I & WHAT AM I WORTH?

I AM A CHILD OF GOD. I AM SO VALUED THAT HE SENT HIS SON TO DIE IN MY PLACE SO THAT I COULD HAVE A RELATIONSHIP WITH HIM.

IN THE GRAND SCHEME OF THINGS I'M WORTHLESS. I'M JUST A HIGHLY FUNCTIONING PIECE OF PROTOPLASM TAKING UP SPACE AND WAITING TO DIE.

WE CAN TRUST THE BIBLE CULTURALLY

The Bible is also deemed untrustworthy today because of its controversial views that seem to go against today's accepted wisdom. For example, the Bible's view on sex and marriage goes against the prevailing view on sexuality in the West. Many are also bothered by the Bible's supposed acceptance of slavery.

When facing cultural challenges to the Bible, it's wise to first understand exactly what the Bible is saying. For example, the type of slavery in the apostles' day bore little resemblance to the slavery practiced in America over the last few hundred years. In their day, slaves were often much more like indentured servants. Though some certainly faced harsh treatment, many were respected in society; they had rights; and they had the ability to eventually earn their freedom. Nowhere does the Bible condone the kidnapping, disregard for life, and ethnic hatred that was practiced in the African slave trade, and attempts to justify racism by appealing to the Bible are wrong. Moreover, the apostles never outright condoned even the type of slavery that was practiced at the time; instead, they simply encouraged

all believers in all situations to be faithful to God.

And yet there are times when the Bible does come face-to-face with cultural norms. For example, while culture might accept all forms of sexuality, the Bible mandates complete purity before marriage and encourages only sex between a husband and wife in marriage. When biblical teaching is in conflict with cultural norms, we must ask whether our cultural beliefs, which vary from nation to nation, have authority over the timeless Word of God, which stands as the truth confronting and critiquing all cultures over all of time.

WE CAN TRUST THE BIBLE SPIRITUALLY

Although we can trust the Bible historically, scientifically, and culturally, the way we come to truly trust the Bible is by reading it. Those who immerse themselves in the Bible with a humble and hungry heart will experience the trustworthiness of the Bible and conclude that the Bible is indeed God's Word, which stands as the final authority over every other authority.

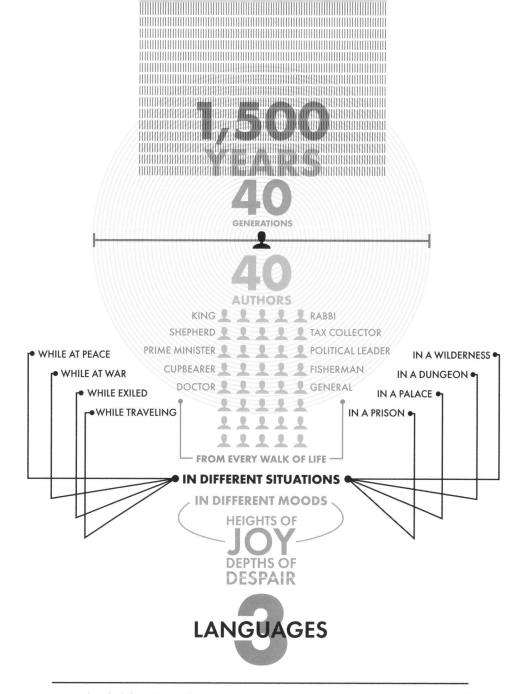

1,500 YEARS

40 GENERATIONS

40 AUTHORS

KING	RABBI
SHEPHERD	TAX COLLECTOR
PRIME MINISTER	POLITICAL LEADER
CUPBEARER	FISHERMAN
DOCTOR	GENERAL

FROM EVERY WALK OF LIFE

WHILE AT PEACE
WHILE AT WAR
WHILE EXILED
WHILE TRAVELING

IN A WILDERNESS
IN A DUNGEON
IN A PALACE
IN A PRISON

IN DIFFERENT SITUATIONS

IN DIFFERENT MOODS

HEIGHTS OF **JOY**
DEPTHS OF DESPAIR

3 LANGUAGES

Yet, the biblical authors spoke with harmony & continuity[10]

THERE IS
ONE
STORY

CHAPTER SIX

WHY SHOULD I STUDY THE BIBLE?

The Bible is a glorious and powerful book. Those who read the Bible in humility and dependence on God find it to be an inexhaustible treasure chest, a fountain for the soul's thirst, and an instrument of supernatural transformation. The Bible is holy and righteous and good.

And yet the Bible can be used in dangerous ways. Many today use the Bible as a self-help book meant to pump up our self-esteem. Others use the Bible as justification for their political agenda. Perhaps more commonly, some religious leaders hold up the Bible merely as a set of rules meant to guide our lives.

The misuse of Scripture is not a recent phenomenon. Jesus scolded the most biblically trained men of his day: "You are in error because you do not know the Scriptures or the power of God" (Matthew 22:29). And Peter warned the churches in his day that there were foolish and ignorant people who twisted the Scriptures to their own destruction (2 Peter 3:16).

So it's important that we approach God's Word with the right motivations. Why should we devote ourselves to studying the Bible?

WHY YOU STUDY THE BIBLE

- KNOW GOD
- KNOW GOD'S WILL
- BECOME GODLY
- BEAR FRUIT
- DEFEND YOURSELF
- FUEL YOUR PRAYERS
- FUEL YOUR JOY

STUDY THE BIBLE TO KNOW GOD

The ultimate goal of studying the Bible is to know the God of the Bible. While we can know something of God's character by observing his creation (Romans 1:20), we cannot experience intimate relationship with God apart from the regular reading and study of the Scriptures.

In his early years, the prophet Samuel heard the voice of God but did not recognize the divine source of that voice. Why? The passage explains: "Now Samuel did not yet know the LORD: The word of the LORD had not yet been revealed to him" (1 Samuel 3:7). Samuel could not know God because he had not yet received his Word.

Unlike Samuel, we are privileged to have God's complete Word available to us. And because we have God's Word, we can know God in intimate relationship. Even beyond the benefits of wisdom and strength that we gain from the Bible, our main pursuit ought to be the knowledge of God, as God speaks through Jeremiah: "Let not the wise boast of their wisdom or the strong boast of their strength or the rich boast of their riches, but let the one who boasts boast about this: that they have the understanding to know me, that I am the LORD" (9:23–24).

KNOW
OD

KNOW
GOD'S WILL

YOU
Y THE
BLE

BECOME
GODLY

BEAR
FRUIT

STUDY THE BIBLE TO KNOW GOD'S WILL

Just as we cannot know the person of God apart from his Word, we also cannot know the will of God apart from his Word. While all people have some understanding of how God wants us to live (Romans 1:14–16), because of our sin, we could not know the full will of God had he not revealed it to us in the Scriptures.

In the Scriptures, we discover how God wants us to relate to him: in loving worship and reverence (Exodus 20:2–7; Matthew 22:37). And we also discover how God wants us to relate to one another: in mutual love that reflects his character (Leviticus 19:18; Matthew 22:39). We find that God desires for us to be sanctified, to flee from sexual immorality (1 Thessalonians 4:3), to be thankful in all circumstances (1 Thessalonians 5:18), to serve others in humility (Ephesians 6:6), and to suffer for his name (1 Peter 2:15).

STUDY THE BIBLE TO BECOME GODLY

As we come to understand the character and will of God, we will be transformed by the renewing of our minds (Romans 12:2). On our own, left in our sinful state, we could not know how to please God (Romans 8:8). But once we know from God's Word how we may please him and look like him, we can begin to look more and more like God and less and less like the world.

Paul told Timothy that all Scripture is useful for "training in righteousness" (2 Timothy 3:16). This means that every single bit of Scripture from Genesis to Revelation is helpful for making us more like God. As we behold God's glory revealed in his Word, we begin to reflect that glory as the Spirit transforms us (2 Corinthians 3:18).

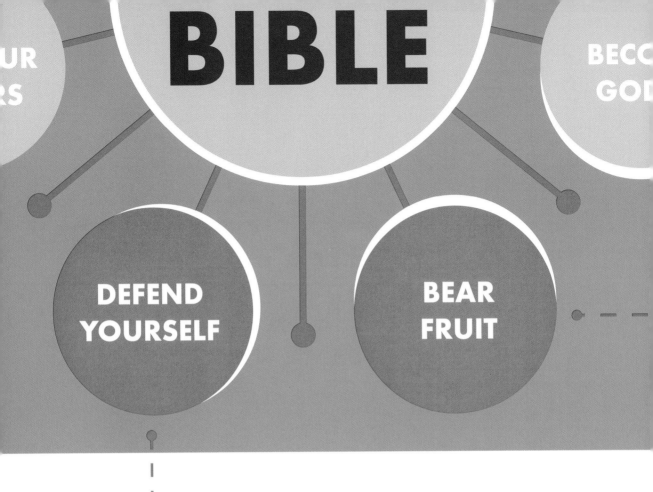

STUDY THE BIBLE TO DEFEND YOURSELF

Studying the Word not only equips us positively to grow in godliness and bear fruit for God but also equips us to fend off the attack of Satan, the spiritual enemy of God and God's people. At the end of his list of spiritual armor in Ephesians 6:17, Paul writes, "Take . . . the sword of the Spirit, which is the word of God." The Word of God functions like a sharp sword that cuts through the binding lies of the enemy.

This is how Jesus employed the Bible against Satan in the wilderness (see Matthew 4:1–11). When the enemy tempted him to redirect his worship away from God, Jesus did not try to fight back with logic or eloquence. Instead, he went immediately to the most potent counterattack and quoted Deuteronomy 6:13: "Worship the Lord your God, and serve him only" (Matthew 4:10).

STUDY THE BIBLE TO BEAR FRUIT

Paul also told Timothy that all Scripture is useful for equipping us for every good work (2 Timothy 3:17). Studying the Word makes us fruitful children who abound in good works and guide others to know him.

This is also the connection that David makes at the beginning of the book of Psalms: "His delight is in the law of the LORD, and on his law he meditates day and night. He is like a tree planted by streams of water that yields its fruit in its season, and its leaf does not wither" (Psalm 1:2–3 ESV). Those who meditate on the Word bear the fruit of the Word. It's no surprise, then, that Jesus says that the one "who hears the word and understands it" ultimately "produces a crop, yielding a hundred, sixty, or thirty times what was sown" (Matthew 13:23).

Knowing the Bible is a prerequisite for fruit bearing. Without the seed of the Word stored in our hearts, we cannot bear fruit for God.

STUDY THE BIBLE TO FUEL YOUR JOY

While Bible study requires diligence and effort, the study of God's Word is not meant to be merely endured but thoroughly enjoyed. By the power of the Spirit, we can experience God's Word for what it really is: "I rejoice in your promise like one who finds great spoil" (Psalm 119:162). So the study of God's Word is not futile busy work; it is a joyful treasure hunt for God's promises.

STUDY THE BIBLE TO FUEL YOUR PRAYERS

One of the greatest difficulties we have with prayer is that as soon as we begin, we don't know what to pray for. After a short laundry list of basic requests, we run out of things to say. The truth is that God has given us an entire library containing a wealth of praises, thanksgivings, and requests to fill our prayers. The Bible is meant to be the foundation and source of confidence for our prayers: "This is the confidence we have in approaching God: that if we ask anything according to his will, he hears us. And if we know that he hears us—whatever we ask—we know that we have what we asked of him" (1 John 5:14–15).

In this way, the Word of God works like fuel for our prayers. Just as steady doses of fuel will increase the intensity and duration of fire, a consistent study of the Word will increase the passion and endurance of our prayer life.

There are countless benefits found in the Bible. And yet these benefits only come to us as we diligently apply our minds and hearts to the study of God's Word. God does not transfer the benefits of knowing the Bible automatically to us when we are saved. Instead, these benefits become ours as we read, observe, interpret, and apply the Bible.

GOD

FUEL
YOUR JOY

WHY YOU STUDY THE BIBLE

FUEL YOUR
PRAYERS

DEFEND
YOURSELF

BEA
FRU

CHAPTER SEVEN

HOW DO I STUDY THE BIBLE?

In order to know the Bible, you must study it diligently. And to study the Bible diligently, you must read it thoroughly. For many, reading through the entire Bible is a daunting task. Since the typical American reads only five books every year, it seems like a stretch for Christians to read the sixty-six books of the Bible each year. But when we put it into perspective, reading the Bible through every year is a very small commitment compared to what we typically give our time to.

For the average reader, it takes about fifteen minutes per day to read through the entire Bible every year.[1] In comparison, the average American adult spends five hours and four minutes per day watching television.[2] So if the average American took just 5 percent of the time that he or she spent watching television and devoted it to Bible reading, they would read through the entire Bible in a year.

So, the Bible is difficult to read, not primarily because it is confusing or hard to read, but because we do not prioritize it.[3] R. C. Sproul agrees: "Here then is the real problem of our negligence. We fail in our duty to study God's Word not so much because it is difficult to understand, not so much because it is dull and boring, but because it is work. Our problem is not a lack of intelligence or a lack of passion. Our problem is that we are lazy."[4]

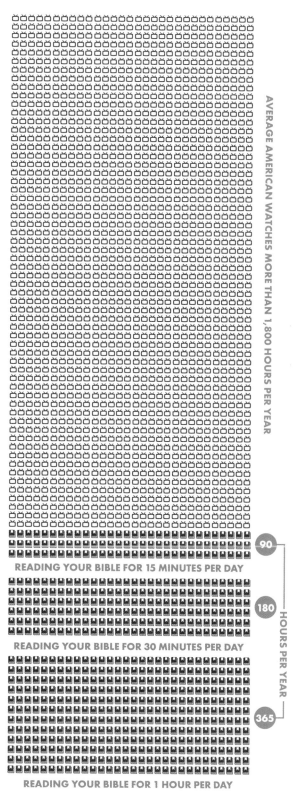

AVERAGE AMERICAN WATCHES MORE THAN 1,800 HOURS PER YEAR

READING YOUR BIBLE FOR 15 MINUTES PER DAY

90

READING YOUR BIBLE FOR 30 MINUTES PER DAY

180

HOURS PER YEAR

READING YOUR BIBLE FOR 1 HOUR PER DAY

365

HOW TO START
READING THE BIBLE

1

**MAKE
TIME**

2

**CHOOSE
A GOOD
TRANSLATION**

3

**FIND
A PLAN**

That's why the first step in reading the Bible is to *make time*. You must decide that consuming God's Word is the highest priority for you, and you must make time for it—or else it will not happen. Choose a consistent time of the day when you will read God's Word. While some are more alert and focused at night, the best time for most people is the morning, since it is the least interruptible and most flexible time of the day.

The second step in reading the Bible is to *choose a good translation*. Some English translations are thought-for-thought translations, which seek to faithfully convey the meaning of each phrase in a way that English readers will best understand. Other English translations are word-for-word translations, which seek to stick to the Hebrew and Greek wording as much as possible, even if it's not as readable in the English. While no translation is perfect, we can be confident in God's Word as we're reading good translations, since these translations are formed by teams of scholars who are well-trained in the original languages.

There is no shortage of English translations to choose from, but some translations are more suitable for daily Bible

reading than others. You want to choose translations that seek to be as close as possible to the original Hebrew and Greek, while also seeking readability in the English. Some good translations you can choose are the New International Version (NIV), the English Standard Version (ESV), and the Christian Standard Bible (CSB).

The third step in Bible reading is to *find a plan*. Because the Bible was given to us as a collection of books, it was meant to be read through book by book. While it may be helpful to read through individual key verses, this kind of reading style gives the impression that we can pick and choose the passages we want to read and avoid the passages we don't. Just as there are countless options for good English translations, there is also an abundance of wonderful Bible reading plans that allow you to go through the entire Bible in a year. Some plans take you through several sections of the Bible each day, while some focus your reading on one book at a time.[5]

Whichever plan you choose, the important thing is to choose a plan that takes you through the entire Bible. Just as with any significant endeavor in life, if you want to develop the habit of reading the Bible each day, you must have a plan.

OBSERVE

INTERPRET

APPLY

MEMORIZE

HOW DO I STUDY THE BIBLE?

WHAT DOES THE PASSAGE SAY?

WHAT DOES THE PASSAGE MEAN?

HOW DOES THE PASSAGE TRANSFORM US?

USE THE PASSAGE OVER & OVER

OBSERVE

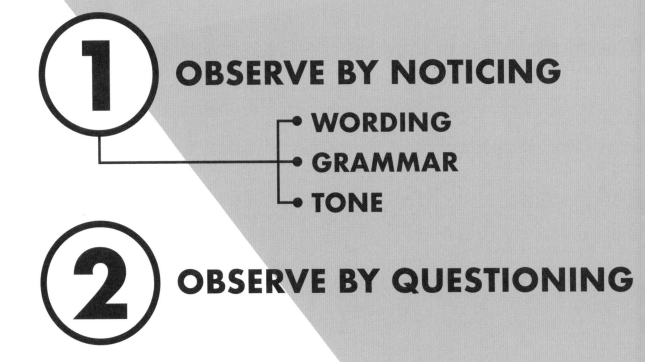

1 OBSERVE BY NOTICING
- WORDING
- GRAMMAR
- TONE

2 OBSERVE BY QUESTIONING

WHAT DOES THE PASSAGE SAY?

Just like any book, the Bible must be read in order to be understood. But unlike most books, the Bible deserves not just to be read but to be deeply studied. While simply reading the Bible will surely benefit our souls, the riches of the Word come to those who study it by observing, interpreting, and applying the Word.

In the *observation* phase of Bible study, we are asking the question, "What does the passage say?" Before discerning what the passage means, we must first understand what it says. This is crucial to understanding the passage. As Howard Hendricks and William Hendricks note, "The quality of your interpretation will always depend on the quality of your observation."[6]

First, we should observe by *noticing*. Mark down anything you notice about the wording, grammar, and tone of the passage. Are there any repeated words? What is the tone of the author? Are there any prepositions, transition words, interjections, or conjunctions?

Second, we should observe by *questioning*. Get curious and write down every question that you can think of about the passage. Does anything confuse you about the passage? Are you unsure about the meaning of a certain word? Do you wonder what an Old Testament allusion or quote is referring to? Jot down all of these thoughts.

It's important to remember that you are asking questions from a place of submission to the Bible and not from a place of suspicion of the Bible. You are not asking questions in order to feed your distrust but to understand the passage so you can feed your worship.

INTERPRET

EXAMINE THE LITERARY CONTEXT

INVESTIGATE THE HISTORICAL CONTEXT

PAY ATTENTION TO THE GENRE

Now that you have spent time observing the passage, you can begin to interpret. In the phase of *interpretation*, you are answering the question, "What does the passage mean?"

To interpret the passage, first pay attention to the *literary context*. The literary context is the location of the passage within the book. For example, the classic "Love Chapter," 1 Corinthians 13, has been read at countless weddings as a passage about marital love. But in the context of 1 Corinthians as a whole, and especially 1 Corinthians 11–14, it is clear that Paul's purpose in 1 Corinthians 13 is to encourage the believers to pursue love even more than pursuing spiritual gifts.

Also pay attention to the *historical context*. The historical context is the location of the passage within the setting in which it was written. Much of the historical context will be contained within the passage or in a footnote. For example, in the story of the woman at Bethany in Mark 14:4–5 (ESV), the disciples say, "Why was the ointment wasted like that? For this ointment could have been sold for more than three hundred denarii and given to the poor." The ESV text note states that a denarius "was a day's wage for a laborer." Knowing this historical context helps you understand that the ointment the woman poured out on Jesus' head could have been sold for nearly a year's salary!

WHAT DOES THE PASSAGE MEAN?

Knowing the literary and historical context, we should also pay attention to the *genre*. For example, it's important to know the difference between a psalm, which is poetry, and a gospel, which is a historical account. When David writes in a psalm, "Smoke rose from [God's] nostrils; consuming fire came from his mouth" (Psalm 18:8), he is using poetic, figurative language. But when John writes in his gospel, "So [Jesus] made a whip out of cords, and drove all from the temple courts" (John 2:15), he is recording what actually happened in history.

Now that you know the literary context, the historical context, and the genre, go back to the questions you asked in the observation phase and see if you can provide answers to your own questions. Another helpful way of summarizing your work of interpretation is to paraphrase the text. Write the whole passage in your own words. Paraphrasing is especially helpful because it forces us to engage with and internalize every word in the verse.

As you answer your questions and paraphrase the text, you're seeking to answer the question, "What is the author's main point?" Your duty in Bible study is not to create meaning but to discover the meaning that God intended to be conveyed through the author of Scripture.

At the end of your interpretation, it's often helpful to consult biblical resources like commentaries, study Bibles, and sermons from sound Bible teachers to ensure you have interpreted the passage rightly.[7] Because we have the Holy Spirit, we have the ability to interpret the passage rightly on our own. But because we still have sin, we can also distort the meaning of the passage on our own. For this reason, it is helpful at the end of our interpretation to lean on the study of fellow believers and ensure that we have the right interpretation.

APPLY
HOW DOES THE PASSAGE TRANSFORM US?

James warns us not to stop our study at the point of interpretation: "Do not merely listen to the word, and so deceive yourselves. Do what it says" (1:22). If we read, observe, and interpret the passage, but do not apply the passage, we are living in self-deception. We believe that we have done something spiritually valuable, but instead, we have prevented the Word from actually transforming our lives. Howard Hendricks and William Hendricks write, "The ultimate goal of Bible study . . . is not to do something to the Bible . . . but to allow the Bible to do something to you."[8]

The application of some passages is easier to discern than others. The application of Philippians 4:6 is obvious: "Do not be anxious about anything, but in every situation, by prayer and petition, with thanksgiving, present your requests to God." But how do you apply the story of Jesus feeding the four thousand in Mark 8:1–10?

We must remember that all Scripture is useful, and therefore all Scripture has application in our lives. But some passages are meant to be applied in our heads; some passages are meant to be applied in our hearts; and other passages are meant to be applied in our hands.

Applying the Word in your *head* means letting the Word shape your mind. To apply the Word in your head, ask these questions:

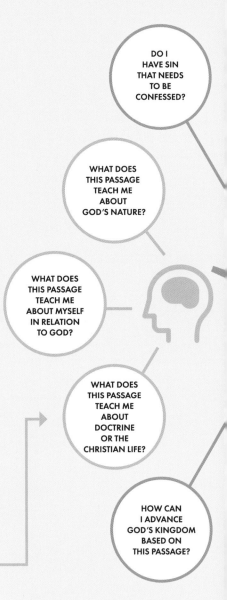

DO I HAVE SIN THAT NEEDS TO BE CONFESSED?

WHAT DOES THIS PASSAGE TEACH ME ABOUT GOD'S NATURE?

WHAT DOES THIS PASSAGE TEACH ME ABOUT MYSELF IN RELATION TO GOD?

WHAT DOES THIS PASSAGE TEACH ME ABOUT DOCTRINE OR THE CHRISTIAN LIFE?

HOW CAN I ADVANCE GOD'S KINGDOM BASED ON THIS PASSAGE?

Even if there isn't an explicit command in the Scripture, we can still apply it. If the Bible is a book about God (which it is), this means that often our application will be discovered as we let Scripture shape our thinking about God.

Applying the Word in your *heart* means letting the Word shape your affections. To apply the Word in your heart, ask these questions:

The Bible often tells us to rejoice, to weep, to be glad, to have thankful hearts. It tells us to love righteousness and hate evil. Sometimes our application will not necessarily be doing something but feeling something in response to Scripture. This doesn't mean that emotions lead the way in Bible study, but it does mean we ought to feel right affections for God in response to his glorious truth.

Applying the Word in your *hands* means letting the Word shape your actions. To apply the Word in your hands, ask these questions:

Sometimes Scripture tells us how to apply it. When the Scriptures clearly tell us to do something, the proper response is to do it. If the Word tells us to actively love our community in Christ, to confess our sins, and to give our possessions generously, the proper response is simply to do it.

If we expand our conception of application to the head, heart, and hands, then we see clearly how all of Scripture is applicable and useful. We may not know what to do in response to Jesus' feeding of the four thousand. But we do know what to think and feel in response: we must acknowledge the compassion, power, and provision of Jesus and joyfully praise him for the ways he displays this in our lives.

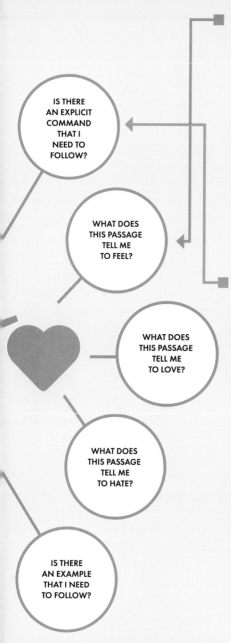

IS THERE AN EXPLICIT COMMAND THAT I NEED TO FOLLOW?

WHAT DOES THIS PASSAGE TELL ME TO FEEL?

WHAT DOES THIS PASSAGE TELL ME TO LOVE?

WHAT DOES THIS PASSAGE TELL ME TO HATE?

IS THERE AN EXAMPLE THAT I NEED TO FOLLOW?

 **HEAD**

 **HEART**

 **HANDS**

ALLOWING THE WORD TO SHAPE MY MIND

- WHAT DOES THIS PASSAGE TEACH ME ABOUT GOD'S NATURE?
- WHAT DOES THIS PASSAGE TEACH ME ABOUT MYSELF IN RELATION TO GOD?
- WHAT DOES THIS PASSAGE TEACH ME ABOUT DOCTRINE OR THE CHRISTIAN LIFE?

ALLOWING THE WORD TO SHAPE MY AFFECTIONS

- WHAT DOES THIS PASSAGE TELL ME TO FEEL?
- WHAT DOES THIS PASSAGE TELL ME TO LOVE?
- WHAT DOES THIS PASSAGE TELL ME TO HATE?

ALLOWING THE WORD TO SHAPE MY ACTIONS

- DO I HAVE SIN THAT NEEDS TO BE CONFESSED?
- IS THERE AN EXPLICIT COMMAND THAT I NEED TO FOLLOW?
- IS THERE AN EXAMPLE THAT I NEED TO FOLLOW?
- HOW CAN I ADVANCE GOD'S KINGDOM BASED ON THIS PASSAGE?

MEMORIZE

There is no greater way to solidify and capitalize on your study of the Bible than to memorize the Scripture you study. Memorizing is one of the most difficult and time-consuming disciplines, and yet it is also one of the most rewarding.

Memorization is storing up God's Word in your heart so that it transforms you. As the psalmist wrote, "I have hidden your word in my heart that I might not sin against you" (Psalm 119:11). Memorization equips you with the Word of God on the go, so that at any time and in every circumstance you can fight against sin and pursue righteousness. By memorizing Scripture, you provide more ammunition for the Spirit to convict, empower, and renew you. There is perhaps no spiritual discipline that reaps more lasting and widespread benefits than Scripture memorization.

As with Bible study, the main obstacle to Bible memorization is not ability but priority. For example, think of how many music lyrics you have memorized. You didn't have to work too hard to store those lyrics up in your heart. You remember them because you love the music. In the same way, if we bring enough love and energy into our Bible study, we will give ourselves the time and energy we need to memorize the Scriptures.

If you want to memorize large chunks of the Bible, you need to develop a system for reviewing Scripture memory and systematically working your way through chunks of the Bible. Andrew Davis's *An Approach to Extended Memorization of Scripture* provides a helpful way to memorize your way through books of the Bible.[9]

USE THE PASSAGE OVER & OVER

1 SAY THE REFERENCE, REPEAT THE REFERENCE

2 REPEAT THE PASSAGE IN SECTIONS: SAY THE PASSAGE IN SEVERAL BITE-SIZED SECTIONS, REPEATING EACH SECTION

3 REPEAT THE REFERENCE AGAIN

4 REVIEW THE PASSAGE SEVERAL MORE TIMES, LENGTHENING THE SECTIONS EACH TIME

5 DISCUSS THE PASSAGE, DISSECT IT, DISCUSS THE MEANING OF WORDS, DISCOVER HOW THE PASSAGE APPLIES TO YOUR LIFE

7 GREAT STUDY BIBLES

	ESV STUDY BIBLE	REFORMATION STUDY BIBLE	NIV STUDY BIBLE	NIV BIBLICAL THEOLOGY STUDY BIBLE	MACARTHUR STUDY BIBLE	CSB STUDY BIBLE	KJV STUDY BI
TRANSLATIONS AVAILABLE	ESV	ESV, NKJV (2016)	NIV	NIV	NIV, ESV NKJV, NASB	CSB	KJV
THEOLOGICAL POSITION	REFORMED	REFORMED	BROAD EVANGELICAL	CONSERVATIVE EVANGELICAL	REFORMED DISPENSATIONAL	CONSERVATIVE EVANGELICAL	REFORMED
PAGE COUNT	2,752	2,560	2,560	2,912	2,208	2,336	2,216
PUBLISHER	CROSSWAY	REFORMATION TRUST	ZONDERVAN	ZONDERVAN	THOMAS NELSON	B&H	REFORMATI HERITAGE
GENERAL EDITOR	WAYNE GRUDEM	R.C. SPROUL	KENNETH L. BARKER	D.A. CARSON	JOHN MACARTHUR	EDWIN A. BLUM	JOEL R. BEEKE
PUBLICATION DATE	2008	1995/2015	1985/2011	2015	2010	2010/2017	2014
BIBLE READING PLAN	YES	YES	NO	NO	YES	YES	YES
ONLINE VERSION AVAILABLE	YES	YES	NO	YES	YES	YES	YES
MOBILE APP AVAILABLE	YES	YES	YES	NO	YES	YES	NO
NUMBER OF STUDY NOTES	19,500	20,000	20,000+	20,000	25,000	15,000+	20,000+
NUMBER OF CHARTS	200+	12	75	60+	177	16	N/A
NUMBER OF MAPS	200+	41	90	90+	87	59	14
NUMBER OF ARTICLES	63	84	7	28	3	24	59
NUMBER OF CONTRIBUTORS	95	75	46	66	10+	71	40+

A WORTHWHILE PURSUIT

Studying the Bible diligently takes serious time and effort. There is no way around it. And yet there is no greater pursuit on earth than knowing God in his Word, and there is no pursuit that is more worthy of our energy.

As Paul told Timothy, "Train yourself to be godly. For physical training is of some value, but godliness has value for all things, holding promise for both the present life and the life to come" (1 Timothy 4:7–8). Pursuing the knowledge of God through Bible study is worth it because while death will end all of our earthly pursuits, the benefits of Bible study will never end.

CHAPTER EIGHT

WHAT IS THE BIBLE ABOUT?

GOD'S CHARACTER

GOD'S WORKS

GOD'S PROMISES

GOD'S PLAN

The Bible is not primarily about us. Above all, the Bible is a book about God. God gave us the Bible so we can observe his character, discover his works, hold on to his promises, and embrace his plan of salvation.

This is good news for you. Though the Bible has much to say about who you are, it is primarily about who God is and what he has done to save you despite who you are. This is why the Scriptures provide great hope. For it's only when you understand who God is and what he has done that you can begin to understand yourself rightly.

When you understand that the Bible is a book about God, then all of Scripture becomes a gold mine for discovering the character and works of God. There are plenty of places in Scripture that don't seem to have immediate implications for us. And yet, because the Bible is a book about God, these sections can become just as useful as the sections for which practical application is obvious.

THE BIBLE IS ABOUT GOD'S PLAN OF SALVATION IN JESUS

The Pharisees, who were the teachers of the Bible during the time of Jesus, knew that the Bible was about God. They studied the Scriptures diligently, memorized the law, and reordered their lives in obedience to it, hoping to reflect the character of their God.

And yet the Pharisees had a major problem. While they searched the Scriptures for God, they missed him. Jesus told them, "You study the Scriptures diligently because you think that in them you have eternal life. These are the very Scriptures that testify about me, yet you refuse to come to me to have life" (John 5:39–40). The Pharisees missed the main point of the Bible because they missed Jesus.

It wasn't just the Pharisees who overlooked Jesus in the Scriptures. Even Jesus' disciples couldn't see their own Lord within the pages of the Old Testament. After his resurrection, Jesus walked with them along the road to Emmaus and helped them see the true nature of the Scriptures: "Beginning with Moses and all the Prophets, he explained to them what was said in all the Scriptures concerning himself" (Luke 24:27).

JESUS
COVER TO COVER

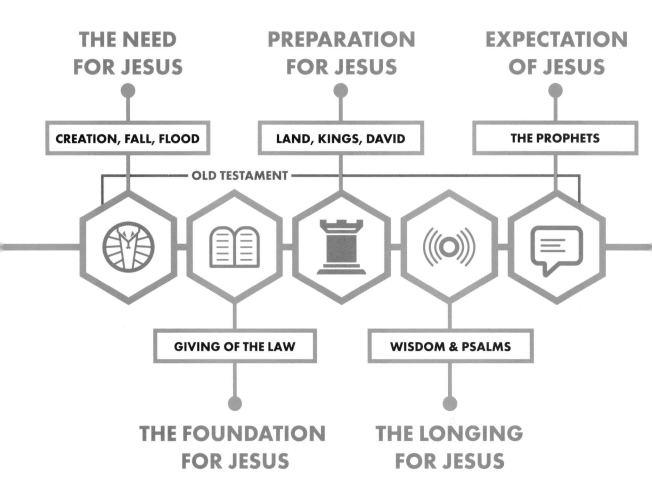

THE NEED FOR JESUS

CREATION, FALL, FLOOD

PREPARATION FOR JESUS

LAND, KINGS, DAVID

EXPECTATION OF JESUS

THE PROPHETS

OLD TESTAMENT

GIVING OF THE LAW

WISDOM & PSALMS

THE FOUNDATION FOR JESUS

THE LONGING FOR JESUS

We, too, miss the main point of the Bible if we fail to see and discover Jesus in all the Scriptures. Yes, the Bible is a book about God. But even more specifically, the Bible is a story about God's plan of salvation for us in Jesus Christ. As we read God's Word from Genesis to Revelation, we discover the Son of God, who came to save us from our sins.

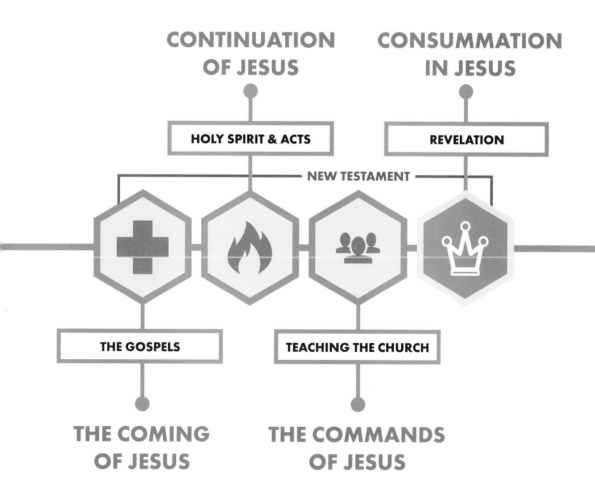

Just as Jesus did with his disciples, we will begin our exploration of God's story with the books of Moses: Genesis, Exodus, Leviticus, Numbers, and Deuteronomy.

THE OLD TESTAMENT

THE NEED FOR JESUS

The first few chapters of the Bible recount God's creation of the heavens and earth, plants and trees, living creatures, and man and woman. It doesn't take long for humanity to sin and fall away from their relationship with God, and the world-sweeping flood shows just how sinful humanity had grown. In this, we see the need for Jesus, the coming offspring who will crush the head of the serpent and do what the flood was unable to do: bring about a new humanity.

THE FOUNDATION FOR JESUS

Then God calls Abram, who would eventually be renamed "Abraham," with a promise of land and offspring: "Go from your country, your people and your father's household to the land I will show you. I will make you into a great nation" (Genesis 12:1–2). The rest of Genesis tells of Abraham's family multiplying and making their way to Egypt, where we find in the book of Exodus that they have been enslaved. Echoing his call to Abraham, God calls Moses to bring his people out of Egypt into the promised land. In the midst of the wilderness on the way to the promised land, God gives his people the law, which they were commanded to obey. Through the call of Abraham, the call of Moses, and the giving of the law, we see the foundation for Jesus, who will fulfill God's promises given to his people and fulfill the law for his people.

PREPARATION FOR JESUS

After the death of Moses, Joshua leads God's people into the promised land. While at first the people seem to have changed their ways in the new land, they eventually turn to wickedness and disorder. They demand to have a king like the other nations, and after King Saul abandons his obligations to God, David and his descendants are promised the crown forever. In this, we see the preparation for Jesus, the descendant of David, who will reign forever over God's people in the new Jerusalem.

THE LONGING FOR JESUS

Israel continues into turmoil, even while holding on to the promise of the Messiah and the restoration of peace. The songs of Israel recorded in the Psalms and the books of Wisdom capture the longing for Jesus. With powerful imagery and metaphor, the people rejoice in God's promises and groan in waiting for a coming Savior who will fulfill them.

EXPECTATION OF JESUS

Out of the chaos and exile of the people, God raises up prophets who expand on and illuminate the promises of a coming Messiah. Isaiah describes him as a Suffering Servant, and Jeremiah and Ezekiel describe him as one who will usher in a new covenant and write God's law on the hearts of God's people. Through the prophets, we see the expectation of Jesus, who will bear the sins of his people in their place.

THE NEW TESTAMENT

THE COMING OF JESUS

The New Testament begins with a declaration of the fulfillment of God's promises in the Old Testament: "This is the genealogy of Jesus the Messiah the son of David, the son of Abraham" (Matthew 1:1). That is, Jesus is the fulfillment of the offspring of Abraham and the reign of David. Throughout the gospel accounts, Jesus shows himself to be the Son of David, who is the King of Israel; the Suffering Servant, who bears the sins of many; and the Son of God, who defeats death and is seated at the right hand of the Father. In Matthew, Mark, Luke, and John, we see the coming of Jesus.

CONTINUATION OF JESUS

Before Jesus ascends to the Father, he gives his disciples a mission: "You will receive power when the Holy Spirit comes on you; and you will be my witnesses in Jerusalem, and in all Judea and Samaria, and to the ends of the earth" (Acts 1:8). The book of Acts records the disciples' obedience to this mission with the power of the Holy Spirit. Though Jesus has ascended to the Father, his work continued through his people as they spread the good news about him. In Acts, the continuation of Jesus is displayed through his apostles and church as they proclaim and display his gospel.[1]

THE COMMANDS OF JESUS

As churches are established in every city, the apostles send letters to guide the body of Christ that has spread throughout the world. From Romans to Jude, the commands of Jesus are laid out, as Jesus shows his people how they are to live and worship in response to his gospel.

CONSUMMATION IN JESUS

The canon closes with the book of Revelation, which gives a stunning picture of the consummation in Jesus. God shows us how all of his promises will be fulfilled and how we will enjoy him and glorify him with our praises forever.

THE BIBLE IS FOR YOU

The Bible is a story about God's plan of salvation in Jesus. It testifies to the need for Jesus, the foundation for Jesus, the preparation for Jesus, the longing for Jesus, the expectation of Jesus, the coming of Jesus, the continuation of Jesus, the commands of Jesus, and the consummation of Jesus. Jesus is the point, from beginning to end.

At the same time, while the Bible is a story about Jesus, the Bible is for you. God gave you this book so you could read it, study it, and, by knowing him through it, enjoy and glorify him forever. The story of the Bible is laid out for you, but you must pick it up and read.

CHAPTER NINE

 **CREATION**  **FALL**  **FLOOD**

THE NEED FOR JESUS

"In the beginning God . . ." (Genesis 1:1). Before anything was, God is. The Bible starts with the presence of God, with no origin or explanation. All of creation has a beginning in Genesis 1, but not God. Out of nothing, he creates the heavens and earth (Genesis 1:2).

THE DAYS OF CREATION

1 LIGHT, HEAVENS & EARTH

2 WATER & ATMOSPHERE

3 DRY LAND & VEGETATION

4 SUN, MOON, & STARS

5 BIRDS & SEA CREATURES

6 LAND ANIMALS & MAN

7 REST

CREATION: JESUS WORKING

FALL: JESUS NEEDED

It's important at the start to understand that the Son of God doesn't come on the scene *later* in the story. No, *at the beginning*, he also was. As the Father spoke and the Spirit hovered (Genesis 1:2), the Creator Son was working in creation.

John tells us, "In the beginning was the Word, and the Word was with God, and the Word was God. He was with God in the beginning. Through him all things were made; without him nothing was made that has been made" (1:1–3).

On the first day, there was light and darkness, day and night. The next day, God created the sky, and on the third, he wrapped up the seas and made room for dry land. As the earth dried up, he called the earth to bring plants and fruit trees. On the fourth day, he ordered the sun, the moon, and the stars to determine days and seasons and years. The fifth day brought sea creatures and birds, and the sixth began with creatures for the earth. Then came the pinnacle of God's creation—man and woman, formed in his image. The last day of the week was set aside for God to rest from his work.

God places the man in the garden to work and keep it. He gives him every tree in the garden to eat but forbids him to eat of the tree of the knowledge of good and evil. The days of creation follow a rhythm: God creates and "God saw that it was good." This continues until Genesis 2:18: "It is not good for the man to be alone. I will make a helper suitable for him." God creates woman and presents her to the man. For some time, they live without shame before one another and before their God (Genesis 2:25).

Sinless joy is cut short when the serpent approaches the woman in the garden. He tempts her to doubt God's Word and eat from the forbidden tree. Desiring the fruit, she eats, disregarding God's command, and gives the fruit to her husband, who does the same.

Immediately, the shame of sin struck them both, and they covered themselves. It's the same shame that makes us hide from God to this day. The Lord arrives and gives the consequences: the woman will suffer pain in childbearing and work

THE BEAUTIFUL TREE

**THE TREE OF KNOWLEDGE OF GOOD & EVIL
GAVE ADAM & EVE THE OPPORTUNITY**
TO EXERCISE THEIR FREE WILL
EVERY TIME THEY WALKED BY THE TREE
AND CHOSE NOT TO EAT
THEY WERE ABLE TO GIVE BACK
THEY WERE ABLE TO SAY TO GOD

I LOVE YOU
I TRUST YOU

against her husband, and the man will toil in pain until his death.

But even before the Lord pronounces judgment on the man and the woman, he gives them a ray of hope.

✚ A RESCUER IS PROMISED

> Cursing the serpent, God tells him, "I will put enmity between you and the woman, and between your offspring and her offspring; he shall bruise your head, and you shall bruise his heel."
> Genesis 3:15 (ESV)

Who is this offspring who will suffer a bruised heel while bruising the head of the serpent? Who is this offspring who will one day crush the curse of sin and return us to God's presence?

Even before God pronounced the curse of sin, God proclaimed the gospel of Jesus. While defeating sin, Jesus would suffer on the cross; while bruising the serpent's head, his heel would be bruised. But the offspring would have the victory. While the serpent took a fatal blow, Jesus' bruised heel would bring the salvation of many (Romans 16:20).

CONSEQUENCES OF THE FALL

BROKEN RELATIONSHIP WITH GOD

MAN NOW HAS A SIN NATURE

ALL CREATION IS UNDER A CURSE

PHYSICAL & SPIRITUAL DEATH

FLOOD: JESUS FORESHADOWED

As Adam and Eve bear children, the stain of sin is seen from the very start. Their firstborn son, Cain, murders their second son, Abel, in a rage of jealousy and is cursed by God. After generation and generation of sin, "the LORD saw how great the wickedness of the human race had become on the earth . . . The LORD regretted that he had made human beings on the earth, and his heart was deeply troubled" (Genesis 6:5–6).

God decides to wipe out all of humanity and every living creature with a flood—except Noah, a righteous man who "found favor in the eyes of the LORD" (Genesis 6:8). He commands Noah to build an ark and bring his family and a pair of every creature into the ark to preserve them from the flood of judgment.

After a forty-day storm and a nearly twelve-month flood, Noah and his family and the animals leave the ark, which had saved them from God's judgment on the earth.

God makes a covenant with Noah and promises to never curse the ground again and never destroy all living creatures, as he had done with the flood. This covenant with Noah continued a long history of covenants that God makes with his people: from Noah to Abraham to Jacob to Moses to David. Just as he had done with Adam, God told Noah to begin a new humanity by being fruitful and multiplying.

And yet, even in the righteous Noah, we begin to see the weakness of the covenant and its failure to produce a new humanity. It's not long before Noah, like Adam, gives himself to sinful desire, and it's not long before some of Noah's descendants are cursed, just as Cain was (Genesis 9:25).

Soon, humanity gathers together and builds a tower to make a name for themselves in defiance against God. Knowing their intentions, God comes down and disperses them across the earth. The history of Adam and Eve has repeated itself yet again, as it will in every generation. The pride of man sets itself up against the knowledge of God, and Almighty God responds with judgment.

Despite Noah's righteousness, despite the ark, and despite the judgment of the worldwide flood, humanity could not rid itself of its greatest problem—sin and death.

All of this points to the need for a Savior to come who, like the ark, would preserve everyone who takes refuge in him and save them from the wrath and judgment of God. There would yet be a Savior who, like Noah, would stand out as righteous in a sinful world. This Savior would not just save people from judgment. By dying for the sins of the world and rising again to life, he would take away their greatest problem—sin and death—and bring them into an everlasting covenant with God.

JESUS
IS GREATER THAN

 ADAM

 NOAH

CHAPTER TEN

ABRAHAM

MOSES

LAW

THE FOUNDATION FOR
JESUS

Even though we are only eleven chapters into the Bible, the need for a Savior is clear. Through Noah and the ark, it appeared that God was bringing a fresh beginning to the earth. But because the flood failed to remove the stain of sin from humanity, history repeats itself, and humanity continues in rebellion against the Word of God.

The Offspring promised to Adam and Eve is yet to come, and the serpent's sin is yet to be bruised. A greater Savior than Noah is needed: one who is without sin, one who preserves humanity from God's wrath, and one who is able to take away the stain of sin. So how will God bring this Offspring and this Savior?

ABRAHAM: THE PROMISE OF OFFSPRING

The story continues with the call of Abram, a distant descendant of Shem, Noah's son: "Go from your country, your people and your father's household to the land I will show you. I will make you into a great nation, and I will bless you; I will make your name great, and you will be a blessing. I will bless those who bless you, and whoever curses you I will curse; and all peoples on earth will be blessed through you" (Genesis 12:1–3).

Holding to God's promise of land, offspring, and blessing, Abram goes out from his hometown in obedience to God. Since Abraham has no son, he wonders how God is going to make "a great nation" out of him. God tells this childless man to look at the stars of heaven and then promises him, "So shall your offspring be" (Genesis 15:5). Abraham believes God's promise that he would bring the promised offspring, and we learn that God "credited it to him as righteousness" (Genesis 15:6).

A few thousand years later, the apostle Paul tells us that this wasn't just written to inform us of God's promise to Abraham, the promise of his son, Isaac. It was foreshadowing for us the way in which we would be counted righteous. Like Abraham, if we believe in the promised Offspring of Abraham, Jesus Christ, we will also have righteousness credited to us (Romans 4:24–25).

In Genesis 17, Abram gets a new name, "Abraham," meaning "father of many." And with this new name, God gives him the sign of circumcision, an outward sign that distinguishes Abraham and his descendants, a sign meant to represent a heart that is set apart for God (Romans 2:28–29). With this new sign, God also promises to bless Abraham and Sarah with a son named Isaac in a year.

God fulfills his promise, and Isaac is born to Abraham. But to test the strength of Abraham's faith, God calls him to sacrifice his son. Abraham obeys God, accompanying Isaac up the mountain of sacrifice, believing that God is always faithful to his promises. God sees Abraham's faith, and instead of requiring the sacrifice of Isaac, he sends a ram to be sacrificed in Isaac's place. God blesses Abraham and reaffirms the promise to make him into a great nation.

So Abraham went as the LORD told him. Genesis 12:4

By faith Abraham, when called to go to a place he would later receive as his inheritance, obeyed and went, even though he did not know where he was going. Hebrews 11:8

why? *Abraham and Sarah knew God would be faithful because he "had made the promise." Hebrews 11:11*

BELIEVED
To have faith - the object of his faith was God

THE **FAITH** OF ABRAHAM

(The Rescuer is foreshadowed again)

ALL PEOPLES ON EARTH WILL BE BLESSED THROUGH YOU

START

The LORD had said to Abram, "Go from your country, your people and your father's household to the land I will show you." Genesis 12:1

After this, the word of the LORD came to Abram in a vision: "Do not be afraid, Abram. I am your shield, your very great reward." But Abram said, "Sovereign LORD, what can you give me since I remain childless…?" [God] took him outside and said, "Look up at the sky and count the stars—if indeed you can count them." Then he said to him, "So shall your offspring be." Abram believed the LORD, and he credited it to him as righteousness. Genesis 15:1–2, 5–6

CREDITED ●────────→ RIGHTEOUSNESS

Settling an account through a payment

Holy, clean, pure, to have a relationship with God

MOSES: THE PROMISE OF DELIVERANCE

As the years pass, God fulfills his promise to multiply Abraham's offspring. Isaac has a son named Jacob, who is nicknamed Israel, and Jacob has twelve sons: Reuben, Simeon, Levi, Judah, Issachar, Zebulun, Dan, Naphtali, Gad, Asher, Joseph, and Benjamin. With each generation, God affirms the promise he had given to Abraham. He blesses Abraham's descendants, multiplying them and making them into a great nation. Israel, the nation of children promised to Abraham, begins to form.

But the rapid growth of Abraham's descendants doesn't come without some conflict in Jacob's family. Joseph's brothers become jealous of his father's favor and sell him to the Midianites, who then sell him to the Egyptians. But God, always faithful to his promises, uses Joseph's plight to bring Israel into the wealth of Egypt and out of a land of famine.

When the book of Exodus begins, the Israelites have grown in number but decreased in position. Because they fill the land, they are put into slavery by the Egyptians, who fear their strength. Just as God used Joseph's position in Egypt to bring Israel out of famine, God uses Moses, an Israelite adopted into Egyptian royalty, to bring Israel out of slavery.

God calls Moses to approach Pharaoh and demand that he release the Israelites. Though Moses hesitates at first, with the strength of God and the help of his brother Aaron, he approaches Pharaoh and speaks the word of the Lord. Pharaoh's repeated refusals are ultimately defeated by God's towering signs and wonders, which culminate in the death of all firstborn sons across Egypt.

Before bringing down the final plague, God tells the Israelites to sacrifice a lamb and brush the blood of the lamb on their doorposts. The promise God makes is that all of those under the blood of the lamb will be saved from death. True to his Word, God destroys all firstborn sons but preserves those who were under the covering of the lamb's blood.

This event, referred to as the Passover, became one of the central events celebrated by God's people. When the Passover lamb delivered Israel from God's final plague, God was giving his people a promise of what was to come. God would send the "Lamb of God," his very Son, to be sacrificed for the sins of the people (see 1 Corinthians 5:7). Just as those under the blood of the lamb were delivered from the final plague, all those who by faith are under the blood of Christ will be delivered from God's wrath in the final judgment.

Moses leads the Israelites out of Egypt and toward the promised land. He shows himself to be a godly, humble, and wise leader. But ultimately, he fails in his main objective to bring the people into the land. When he strikes the rock to bring out water for Israel, he disobeys God's command to bring out water by speaking to the rock (Numbers 20:8–12). Besides this, he oversees Israel as they allow fear to keep them from entering the promised land (Numbers 13:25–33). As a result, Moses is forbidden to enter the land, and Israel is punished with forty years of wandering in the wilderness.

While Moses successfully leads Israel out of Egypt, his failures highlight the ongoing need for a greater Deliverer—Jesus Christ. By his death and resurrection, Jesus would not only deliver his people out of their bondage to sin, but he would bring them victoriously into the Promised Land, a new heaven and a new earth—a redeemed world cleansed from the stain of sin. The promise of deliverance through Moses is ultimately fulfilled in Jesus, the Rock who is struck for the salvation of many.

IS GREATER THAN

 **ADAM**

 **NOAH**

 **ABRAHAM**

MOSES

THE PASSOVER LAMB

one-year-old male

EXODUS 12:3 **TAKE A LAMB**

no defects

DON'T BREAK ANY BONES *EXODUS 12:46*

"The blood will be a sign for you on the houses where you are, and when I see the blood, I will pass over you. No destructive plague will touch you when I strike Egypt."
Exodus 12:13

EXODUS 12:46 **EAT THE LAMB IN ONE HOUSE**

EXODUS 12:6 **14TH DAY OF THE 1ST MONTH**

KILL AT TWILIGHT *EXODUS 12:6*

While providing visual symbolism,
the detailed instructions foreshadowed Jesus
and provided a way for God's people to
demonstrate their trust and faith in God.

EXODUS 12:7 **APPLY BLOOD TO DOORFRAME**

And the LORD said to Moses, "Go to the people and consecrate them today and tomorrow. Have them wash their clothes and be ready by the third day, because on that day the LORD will come down on Mount Sinai in the sight of all the people.

Put limits for the people around the mountain and tell them, 'Be careful that you do not approach the mountain or touch the foot of it. Whoever touches the mountain is to be put to death.'"

Exodus 19:10–12

BECAUSE GOD IS HOLY

 WE MUST BE PURE BEFORE HIM

 UNTOUCHED BY SIN

 TO APPROACH HIM UNCLEAN MEANS DEATH

THE LAW: THE PROMISE OF RIGHTEOUSNESS

As the Israelites are brought out of the tyranny of Egypt, in the midst of the wilderness, the LORD calls his people to belong to him exclusively on Mount Sinai: "You yourselves have seen what I did to Egypt, and how I carried you on eagles' wings and brought you to myself. Now if you obey me fully and keep my covenant, then out of all nations you will be my treasured possession. Although the whole earth is mine, you will be for me a kingdom of priests and a holy nation" (Exodus 19:4–6).

To distinguish his people from all other nations on the earth, God gives them the law, first written on tablets in the Ten Commandments.

The Ten Commandments begin with a declaration of God's relationship with his people: "I am the LORD your God, who brought you out of Egypt, out of the land of slavery" (Exodus 20:2). This is how God always gives commands to his covenant people. The demand for obedience follows the act of deliverance.

The first four commandments deal with the people's vertical relationship with God: they cannot put any gods before the Lord; they cannot make a carved image of the Lord; they cannot take the name of the Lord in vain; and they must devote the seventh day to the Lord as a holy day of worship.

The next six commandments deal with the people's horizontal relationships with one another: they were to honor their parents, not murder, not commit adultery, not steal, not bear false witness, and not covet one another's spouse or possessions.

The people are confident they will be able to obey God's voice and receive his blessing. They tell Moses, "We will do everything the LORD has said; we will obey" (Exodus 24:7).

But it doesn't take long for the people to disobey God and fall short of the law's demands. Just a few chapters later, as Moses is on the mountain receiving the word of the Lord, the people grow impatient and decide to take matters into their own hands: "Come, make us gods who will go before us. As for this fellow Moses who brought us up out of Egypt, we don't know what has happened to him" (Exodus 32:1).

10 RULES

FOR RELATIONSHIP WITH GOD

THE FAILURES OF ISRAEL & THE FULFILLMENT OF JESUS

THE ISRAELITES SECRETLY DID THINGS AGAINST THE LORD THEIR GOD THAT WERE NOT RIGHT. FROM WATCHTOWER TO FORTIFIED CITY THEY BUILT THEMSELVES HIGH PLACES IN ALL THEIR TOWNS. THEY SET UP SACRED STONES AND ASHERAH POLES ON EVERY HIGH HILL AND UNDER EVERY SPREADING TREE. AT EVERY HIGH PLACE THEY BURNED INCENSE, AS THE NATIONS WHOM THE LORD HAD DRIVEN OUT BEFORE THEM HAD DONE. THEY DID WICKED THINGS THAT AROUSED THE LORD'S ANGER. THEY WORSHIPED IDOLS, THOUGH THE LORD HAD SAID, "YOU SHALL NOT DO THIS."

2 KINGS 17:9–12

HEAR THE WORD OF THE LORD, YOU ISRAELITES, BECAUSE THE LORD HAS A CHARGE TO BRING AGAINST YOU WHO LIVE IN THE LAND: "THERE IS NO FAITHFULNESS, NO LOVE, NO ACKNOWLEDGMENT OF GOD IN THE LAND. THERE IS ONLY CURSING, LYING AND MURDER, STEALING AND ADULTERY; THEY BREAK ALL BOUNDS, AND BLOODSHED FOLLOWS BLOODSHED.

HOSEA 4:1–2

RELATIONSHIP WITH GOD

YOU SHALL HAVE NO OTHER GODS BEFORE ME	**1** JESUS HAD NO OTHER GODS
YOU SHALL NOT MAKE FOR YOURSELF AN IDOL	**2** JESUS DID NOT MAKE FOR HIMSELF AN IDOL
YOU SHALL NOT MISUSE THE NAME OF THE LORD	**3** JESUS DID NOT MISUSE THE NAME OF THE LORD
REMEMBER THE SABBATH DAY BY KEEPING IT HOLY	**4** JESUS KEPT THE SABBATH DAY HOLY
HONOR YOUR FATHER AND YOUR MOTHER	**5** JESUS HONORED HIS FATHER AND MOTHER
YOU SHALL NOT MURDER	**6** JESUS DID NOT COMMIT MURDER
YOU SHALL NOT COMMIT ADULTERY	**7** JESUS DID NOT COMMIT ADULTERY
YOU SHALL NOT STEAL	**8** JESUS DID NOT STEAL
YOU SHALL NOT GIVE FALSE TESTIMONY	**9** JESUS DID NOT GIVE FALSE TESTIMONY
YOU SHALL NOT COVET	**10** JESUS DID NOT COVET

WHAT WAS THE PURPOSE OF THE TEN COMMANDMENTS & THE LAW?

RELATIONSHIP WITH MAN

FIRST, IT WAS AN INDICATION OF WHAT HOLINESS TRULY WAS AND WHAT IT WOULD REQUIRE TO BE IN RELATIONSHIP WITH GOD. IN THIS WAY THE LAW FUNCTIONED LIKE A MIRROR SHOWING ISRAEL THAT IN THEIR SINFUL CONDITION THEY COULD NOT EXPECT TO FULFILL IT PERFECTLY.

SECONDLY, THE LAW WAS INTENDED TO GUIDE US AS A WAY OF LIVING. THOUGH SALVATION IS NOT ACQUIRED THROUGH THE KEEPING OF THE LAW, FOLLOWING ITS COMMANDS WILL PLEASE GOD.

"DO NOT THINK THAT I HAVE COME TO ABOLISH THE LAW OR THE PROPHETS; I HAVE NOT COME TO ABOLISH THEM BUT TO FULFILL THEM."

MATTHEW 5:17

BEFORE THE COMING OF THIS FAITH, WE WERE HELD IN CUSTODY UNDER THE LAW, LOCKED UP UNTIL THE FAITH THAT WAS TO COME WOULD BE REVEALED. SO THE LAW WAS OUR GUARDIAN UNTIL CHRIST CAME THAT WE MIGHT BE JUSTIFIED BY FAITH. NOW THAT THIS FAITH HAS COME, WE ARE NO LONGER UNDER A GUARDIAN.

GALATIANS 3:23–25

THEREFORE, SINCE WE HAVE A GREAT HIGH PRIEST WHO HAS ASCENDED INTO HEAVEN, JESUS THE SON OF GOD, LET US HOLD FIRMLY TO THE FAITH WE PROFESS. FOR WE DO NOT HAVE A HIGH PRIEST WHO IS UNABLE TO EMPATHIZE WITH OUR WEAKNESSES, BUT WE HAVE ONE WHO HAS BEEN TEMPTED IN EVERY WAY, JUST AS WE ARE—YET HE DID NOT SIN.

HEBREWS 4:14–15

Now if you obey me fully and keep my covenant . . .

IF

THEN

. . . out of all nations you will be my treasured possession. Although the whole earth is mine, you will be for me a kingdom of priests and a holy nation.

Exodus 19:5–6

Aaron, the brother of Moses and a man who once stood boldly for the Lord in the face of Pharaoh, now blasphemes the Lord before his own people by carving a golden calf for the people to worship. The people act just like their father Adam, defying God's trustworthy commands.

When Moses comes down from the mountain and sees the rebellion of the people, he furiously throws down the tablets of the law at the foot of the mountain and breaks them.

The people had assumed that obeying the law would bring them life, as God had said: "Keep my decrees and laws, for the person who obeys them will live by them. I am the LORD" (Leviticus 18:5). But it didn't take long for the people to realize that because they couldn't keep the law, they also couldn't have life through the law. The people wanted God's blessing through the righteousness of the law, but the stain of their sin kept them from enjoying its blessings. Though the law clarified God's demands, it could not empower obedience. Even the law itself anticipated the people's inability to obey it fully, as it commanded the people to make sacrifices to atone for their sins.

If righteousness and life were not to come through the law, how then could God's people ever enjoy God's presence and blessings?

We soon learn that God's plan all along was to give his people life through faith rather than through the law. By grace through faith, God unites us with Christ and fills us with his Spirit, giving us power to obey his commands (Romans 8:4). Remember, Abraham was brought into relationship with God before the law was given. How? By believing in God's promise to bring an offspring. Abraham believed God, and his belief was credited to him as righteousness.

God gave his people the law so they could know they were trapped in their sin and to help them see their need for a Savior. The law "was added because of transgressions until the Seed to whom the promise referred had come" (Galatians 3:19).

Who was this Seed? Over a thousand years after the law was given to Israel, the Fulfillment of the Law, a man named Jesus of Nazareth, arrived among Israel: "Do not think that I have come to abolish the Law or the Prophets; I have not come to abolish them but to fulfill them" (Matthew 5:17). Paul tells us what this means for us: "But now apart from the law the righteousness of God has been made known, to which the Law and the Prophets testify. This righteousness is given through faith in Jesus Christ to all who believe" (Romans 3:21–22).

The law given to Moses and Israel points to a future day when the law is fulfilled in Christ, when God's righteousness is graciously given through faith, and when God's people are empowered to obey God's law by God's Spirit within them.

Can we know God and enjoy his blessings despite our disobedience to the law? Yes. Believe in the One who fulfilled the law and bore our sins. We enjoy the blessings of his obedience on earth because he suffered the curse of our disobedience on the cross.

For whoever keeps the whole law and yet stumbles at just one point is guilty of breaking all of it.
James 2:10

CHAPTER ELEVEN

LAND

JUDGES

KINGS

PREPARATION FOR
JESUS

With the death of Moses, a new leader is appointed—Joshua, a faithful and courageous Israelite. After the Israelites wander for forty years in the wilderness, it looks as though a new era is on the horizon as the descendants of Abraham prepare to enter the land God has promised.

But the Israelites soon find that even life in the promised land does not provide them with an enduring hope. The sin that plagued them in the wilderness continues to plague them in the new land. The kingdom they had hoped for is not yet fulfilled. They need a Leader who has no sin to bring them into the land of abundance, and they need a King who will reign over a kingdom that will never end.

LAND: THE KINGDOM PREPARED

Joshua brings the people of God into the land of God's promise, and he reminds them of the task God gave to Moses while on the plains of Moab: "When you cross the Jordan into Canaan, drive out all the inhabitants of the land before you. Destroy all their carved images and their cast idols, and demolish all their high places" (Numbers 33:51–52). To establish a holy nation, Israel was to drive out the people of the land. If they allow the people to remain in the land, their false gods will drag Israel away from faithfully worshiping the Lord.

The conquest of the promised land at first seems hopeful, as Israel overtakes Jericho with the help of Rahab, a prostitute in the land who feared the Lord. God causes the walls of Jericho to collapse as the people take a lap around the city for seven days and shout, showing that just as it was God's power that brought them out of Egypt, it will be God's power that brings them into the new land.

Yet the promise of a new era for God's people soon falls short of complete fulfillment. Achan, an Israelite, disobeys God by taking some of the objects devoted for destruction by the Lord, keeping them for himself. For this sin, "the LORD's anger burned against Israel" (Joshua 7:1), and the Lord brings judgment on its army. While Joshua and Israel are often victorious in their battles, by the time Joshua is old, there is much land remaining to be conquered. In the end, the conquest of the land is incomplete, as is the hoped-for renewal of Israel and her people.[1]

After Joshua divides up the land according to the tribes of Israel, he gathers Israel together for one final speech. He reminds them of God's grace and power in delivering them from Egypt. He reminds them of how the Lord brought them victory in battle. In light of what God has done for them, he exhorts them, "Now fear the LORD and serve him with all faithfulness. Throw away the gods your ancestors worshiped beyond the Euphrates River and in Egypt, and serve the LORD. But if serving the LORD seems undesirable to you, then choose for yourselves this day whom you will serve" (Joshua 24:14–15).

The people agree with Joshua, and quickly commit their allegiance to the Lord: "We too will serve the LORD, because he is our God" (Joshua 24:18).

Joshua is not naive. He has heard this story already. He was there when Israel committed to obeying the law and then carved a golden calf to worship. He was there when the law failed to remove the sin of the people. He was there when Achan disobeyed God and stole the devoted things, right after the Lord had

TAKING THE LAND
(AN INCOMPLETE CONQUEST)

graciously given them favor in battle. When the people declare their commitment to God, instead of replying with flattery or encouragement, Joshua gives them the harsh truth: "You are not able to serve the LORD. He is a holy God" (Joshua 24:19).

GAZA

The people "are not able to serve the LORD." And throughout the remainder of Israel's history recorded in the Old Testament, Joshua's statement will be proven true again and again. Israel's brief period of conquest and moderate peace is followed by rebellion, tyranny, and idolatry. The people have gained the promised land, but they have not yet received the promised Savior. They need a leader who is greater than Joshua, one who is able to give them a new home and new hearts.

KADESH-BARNEA

SOUTHERN CAMPAIGN

5 Israelites in party with Gibeonites attack Amorite coalition • 9:1–10:10

6 Amorites flee to Valley of Aijalon, where the sun stands still • 10:11–14

7 Capture and destruction of the city of Makkedah • 10:16–28

8 War is waged against the city of Libnah • 10:29–30

9 Lachish is besieged and king of Gezer is destroyed • 10:31–33

10 City of Eglon is taken • 10:34–35

11 Hebron is attacked • 10:36–37

12 Debir is conquered • 10:38–39

13 Joshua defeats the Canaanites from Kadesh-Barnea to Gaza • 10:41

NORTHERN CAMPAIGN

14 Israel surprises Northern coalition by the waters of Merom • 11:7

15 Israel pursues retreating enemy to Sidon and the Valley of Mizpah • 11:8–9

16 Joshua turns back and takes Hazor • 11:10

SIDON

VALLEY OF MIZPAH

MEROM

HAZOR

HILL COUNTRY
OF ISRAEL

SEA OF GALILEE

JORDAN VALLEY

VALLEY OF AIJALON

GIBEON

AI

MAIN FORCE

LOWLAND

MAKKEDAH?

AMBUSH FORCE

EGLON

LACHISH

LIBNAH

JERICHO

GILGAL

GOSHEN

HILL COUNTRY

HEBRON

SHITTIM

DEBIR

SOUTHLAND

10 MILES
16 KM

DEAD SEA

CENTRAL CAMPAIGN

1 Joshua sends spies to Jericho • 2:1–24

2 Israelite camp is established at Gilgal • 4:19

3 Jericho falls, opening the way into Canaan • 6:1–27

4 Battle of Ai – Initial attack fails, but ambush defeats the city • 8:1–29

JOSHUA 24:18–19

NAME

Israel

COMMENTS

We too will serve the LORD, because he is our God.

SUBMIT

⚠ **INVALID VALUE**
You are not able to serve the LORD.
He is a holy God.

JUDGES: THE KINGDOM POLLUTED

While the death of Moses brought a brief period of relative obedience and peace, the death of Joshua ignited a long period of chaos. The people's intention to obey the Lord in Joshua's day quickly gives way to their unrestrained desires. They may be free from the bondage of physical slavery in Egypt, but they are now trapped in spiritual slavery to their sin.

The people not only abandon the Lord, but they also replace him with other gods, the "Baals" whom the foreign peoples who remain in the land serve (Judges 2:11). Generations pass, and they forget the God who brought them out of Egypt, who delivered them from slavery, who brought them into the promised land. And as the people forget the Lord, God's promise to Moses comes true: "If you ever forget the LORD your God and follow other gods and worship and bow down to them, I testify against you today that you will surely be destroyed. Like the nations the LORD destroyed before you, so you will be destroyed for not obeying the LORD your God" (Deuteronomy 8:19–20).

Instead of conquering the foreign nations in the land, Israel is the one conquered as their allegiance to God is replaced by rampant idolatry. Instead of spreading the name of the one true God, the worship of foreign gods spreads throughout Israel. Instead of obeying God and receiving blessing, the people rebel against God and are cursed. They turn away from the Lord and his blessings, and just as he promised, they once again find themselves in peril.

Despite his people's rebellion, the Lord has compassion on them. Instead of allowing his people to suffer under his wrath, as they deserve, he is moved to action on their behalf. He raises up for his people military leaders called "judges," leaders who fight for the people and deliver them from their enemies. Why does the Lord do this? "The LORD relented because of their groaning under those who oppressed and afflicted them" (Judges 2:18).

From Othniel to Ehud, to Deborah and Barak, all the way to Gideon and Samson, the judges whom the Lord raises up provide temporary deliverance for the people of Israel. For a time, the people live in thankfulness and obedience, remembering the consequences of their sin and the deliverance of their God. But the changes were fleeting: "But when the judge died, the people returned to ways even more corrupt than those of their ancestors, following other gods and serving and worshiping them. They refused to give up their evil practices and stubborn ways" (Judges 2:19).

In Samson, we see how even the judges could not fully obey the Lord. Just like the people of Israel, Samson is blessed and favored by the Lord, equipped to obey the Lord, and called to be separate from the ungodly people of the land. But he is enslaved by his lusts, and his sinful desire leads him to choose disobedience and death over obedience and life.

The people need a Judge, a Deliverer, who is able to free them from the peril of their enemies and the plague of their sin. They need a Judge who walks in sinlessness and has the power to lead them to obedience. They need a Judge who will provide not just temporary peace and temporary life, but who can secure both eternal peace and eternal life.

The book of Judges demonstrates Israel's need for a deliverer and foreshadows the One to come—Jesus, who delivers the people from their rebellious hearts and promises to bring a kingdom that will be free from all oppression.

JESUS
IS GREATER THAN

 ADAM

 NOAH

 ABRAHAM

 MOSES

 THE JUDGES

THE JUDGES OF ISRAEL
& THE CYCLE OF SIN

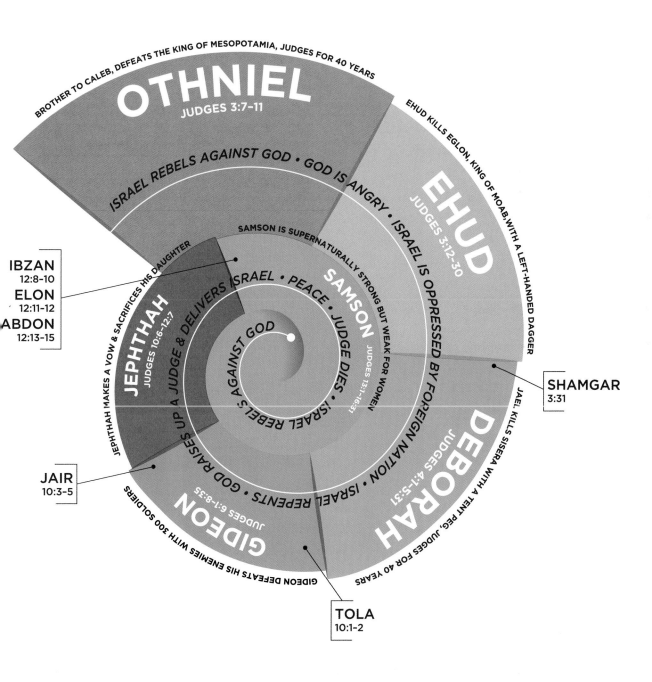

BROTHER TO CALEB, DEFEATS THE KING OF MESOPOTAMIA, JUDGES FOR 40 YEARS

OTHNIEL
JUDGES 3:7-11

EHUD KILLS EGLON, KING OF MOAB, WITH A LEFT-HANDED DAGGER

EHUD
JUDGES 3:12-30

ISRAEL REBELS AGAINST GOD • GOD IS ANGRY • ISRAEL IS OPPRESSED BY FOREIGN NATION • ISRAEL REPENTS • GOD RAISES UP A JUDGE & DELIVERS ISRAEL • PEACE • JUDGE DIES • ISRAEL REBELS AGAINST GOD

SAMSON IS SUPERNATURALLY STRONG BUT WEAK FOR WOMEN

SAMSON
JUDGES 13:1-16:31

IBZAN
12:8-10

ELON
12:11-12

ABDON
12:13-15

JEPHTHAH MAKES A VOW & SACRIFICES HIS DAUGHTER

JEPHTHAH
JUDGES 10:6-12:7

JAIR
10:3-5

GIDEON
JUDGES 6:1-8:35

GIDEON DEFEATS HIS ENEMIES WITH 300 SOLDIERS

TOLA
10:1-2

JAEL KILLS SISERA WITH A TENT PEG, JUDGES FOR 40 YEARS

DEBORAH
JUDGES 4:1-5:31

SHAMGAR
3:31

KINGS: THE KINGDOM PROMISED

During the period of the judges, the Lord brought a loyal Moabite widow named Ruth and her mother-in-law, Naomi, into the small rural town of Bethlehem. Because of God's favor on her, Ruth meets one of her husband's relatives, a man named Boaz, who marries her and redeems her from her widowhood. They have a son named Obed, who eventually has a son named Jesse, who eventually has a son named David, who eventually becomes the king of Israel and the ancestor of Jesus, the promised King of kings.

But David's path to the throne was far from smooth sailing. After a long period of unrest without an official ruler, the people go to Samuel, the nation's most famous prophet, and demand a king, just like the other nations have. Reluctantly, Samuel agrees to appoint a king for them, and with the Lord's guidance, he chooses Saul the Benjaminite. Their first king had all of the kingly features that Israel was looking for: "Kish had a son named Saul, as handsome a young man as could be found anywhere in Israel, and he was

a head taller than anyone else" (1 Samuel 9:2). Even Samuel was stunned at his prowess: "Do you see the man the LORD has chosen? There is no one like him among all the people" (1 Samuel 10:24).

While Saul was flawless on the outside, it didn't take long for his inner flaws to be revealed. After a few military victories, Saul disobeys the Lord by performing an unlawful sacrifice. Such sinful disobedience prompts the Lord to appoint a new king. In contrast to Saul's kingly appearance, the Lord chooses David, a shepherd and the youngest of Jesse's sons.

In its battle with the Philistines, Israel faces doom as their enemy's mightiest soldier, Goliath, challenges Israel to a one-on-one, winner-take-all battle. As all of Israel's men tremble in fear, David leaves his sheep behind and steps up to fight. Where Saul took matters into his own hands and disobeyed the Lord, David humbly depends on the Lord for the victory and trusts in his word: "The LORD who rescued me from the paw of the lion and the paw of the bear will rescue me from the hand of this Philistine" (1 Samuel 17:37). With the sling of one stone and the power of the Lord, David kills the armored giant.

David's victory ensures that he will eventually take the throne from Saul. But Saul would not give up his crown without a fight. For years, Saul sinfully chases David, and David eludes him. The struggle with Saul ends when the Philistines, whom David had triumphantly conquered, wound Saul in battle, who then takes his sword and falls on it. After the death of Saul and a brief period of division in the kingdom under the reign of Saul's son, David is anointed king of Israel.

After the kingdom is united under David, he begins his reign by bringing the ark of God back to Israel, signaling a new era of blessing from the Lord. The Lord confirms this by making a covenant with David: "When your days are over and you rest with your ancestors, I will raise up your offspring to succeed you, your own flesh and blood, and I will establish his kingdom . . . Your house and your kingdom will endure forever before me; your throne will be established forever" (2 Samuel 7:12, 16). God's promise to Abraham to make him into a great nation is now being fulfilled through David, whose descendants will always be on the throne of God's kingdom.

JESUS
IS GREATER THAN

 ADAM

 NOAH

 ABRAHAM

 MOSES

 THE JUDGES

 THE KINGS

As the years and generations pass, we see God's promise to David come true. David experiences unsurpassed military success, and his reign is celebrated throughout the kingdom. When he dies, his son Solomon takes the throne and brings a glorious period of wealth and peace in Israel. Just as God promised, Solomon builds a temple for the Lord, and the Lord builds a Davidic dynasty that doesn't end. Even through the turmoil of Israel after Solomon's reign, God keeps one of David's descendants on the throne.

But even though many of God's promises come true during this period of Israel's history, many remain to be fulfilled. Although David is a man after God's heart, he disobeys God by committing adultery and murder, not long after the promises are given to him. During his reign, David experiences betrayal and treason within his own family, and there is a struggle for power after his death. David's grandson rules Israel with folly, which leads to the kingdom being split in two. And during the reign of Jehoiachin, Israel is captured by Babylon and sent into exile away from the land.

Throughout this chaos, God raises up prophets like Elijah and Elisha to remind the people of the promises of God and to exhort them to return to the Lord their God. Even in the darkest times in Israel, God speaks and moves and works in power.

In truth, Israel's sin and rebellion and division and exile could not prevent God from keeping his promise to David. David's kingdom may be plundered, and Israel may have forgotten their God, but one day, God would raise up a Son of David to take the throne and rule. This King would unite God's children together in peace. This King would lead the people in honor and faithfulness.[2]

AND JUST AS
GOD PROMISED
HIS THRONE WOULD
LAST FOREVER AND EVER

THE KINGS & PROPHETS OF ISRAEL & JUDAH

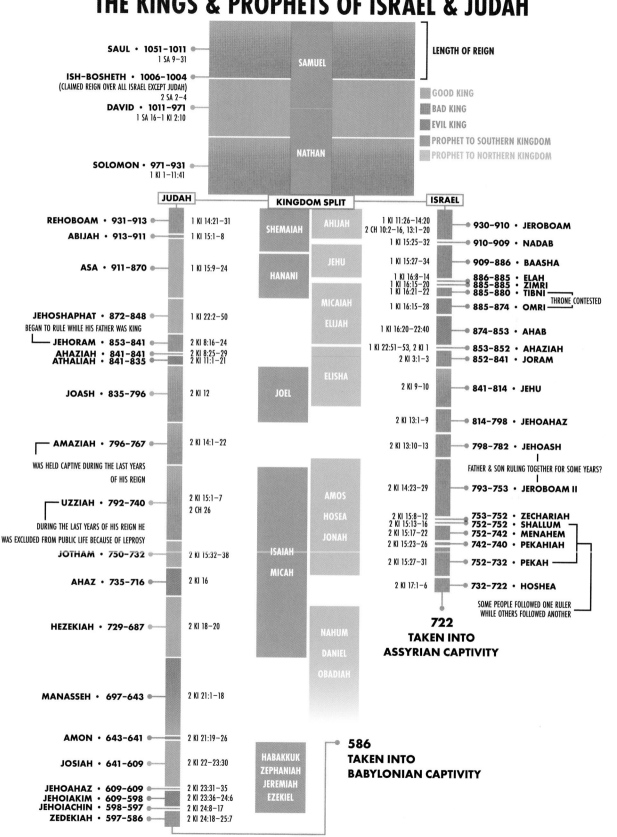

LENGTH OF REIGN

SAUL • 1051–1011
1 SA 9–31

ISH-BOSHETH • 1006–1004
(CLAIMED REIGN OVER ALL ISRAEL EXCEPT JUDAH)
2 SA 2–4

DAVID • 1011–971
1 SA 16–1 KI 2:10

SAMUEL

NATHAN

SOLOMON • 971–931
1 KI 1–11:41

GOOD KING
BAD KING
EVIL KING
PROPHET TO SOUTHERN KINGDOM
PROPHET TO NORTHERN KINGDOM

JUDAH   **KINGDOM SPLIT**   **ISRAEL**

JUDAH		ISRAEL
REHOBOAM • 931–913 — 1 KI 14:21–31	SHEMAIAH / AHIJAH	1 KI 11:26–14:20 / 2 CH 10:2–16, 13:1–20 — 930–910 • JEROBOAM
ABIJAH • 913–911 — 1 KI 15:1–8		1 KI 15:25–32 — 910–909 • NADAB
ASA • 911–870 — 1 KI 15:9–24	HANANI / JEHU	1 KI 15:27–34 — 909–886 • BAASHA
		1 KI 16:8–14 — 886–885 • ELAH
		1 KI 16:15–20 — 885–885 • ZIMRI
		1 KI 16:21–22 — 885–880 • TIBNI — THRONE CONTESTED
	MICAIAH	1 KI 16:15–28 — 885–874 • OMRI
JEHOSHAPHAT • 872–848 — 1 KI 22:2–50	ELIJAH	1 KI 16:20–22:40 — 874–853 • AHAB
BEGAN TO RULE WHILE HIS FATHER WAS KING		
JEHORAM • 853–841 — 2 KI 8:16–24		1 KI 22:51–53, 2 KI 1 — 853–852 • AHAZIAH
AHAZIAH • 841–841 — 2 KI 8:25–29		2 KI 3:1–3 — 852–841 • JORAM
ATHALIAH • 841–835 — 2 KI 11:1–21	ELISHA	
JOASH • 835–796 — 2 KI 12	JOEL	2 KI 9–10 — 841–814 • JEHU
		2 KI 13:1–9 — 814–798 • JEHOAHAZ
AMAZIAH • 796–767 — 2 KI 14:1–22		2 KI 13:10–13 — 798–782 • JEHOASH
WAS HELD CAPTIVE DURING THE LAST YEARS OF HIS REIGN		FATHER & SON RULING TOGETHER FOR SOME YEARS?
		2 KI 14:23–29 — 793–753 • JEROBOAM II
UZZIAH • 792–740 — 2 KI 15:1–7 / 2 CH 26	AMOS / HOSEA / JONAH	
DURING THE LAST YEARS OF HIS REIGN HE WAS EXCLUDED FROM PUBLIC LIFE BECAUSE OF LEPROSY		2 KI 15:8–12 — 753–752 • ZECHARIAH
		2 KI 15:13–16 — 752–752 • SHALLUM
		2 KI 15:17–22 — 752–742 • MENAHEM
		2 KI 15:23–26 — 742–740 • PEKAHIAH
JOTHAM • 750–732 — 2 KI 15:32–38	ISAIAH / MICAH	2 KI 15:27–31 — 752–732 • PEKAH
AHAZ • 735–716 — 2 KI 16		2 KI 17:1–6 — 732–722 • HOSHEA
		SOME PEOPLE FOLLOWED ONE RULER WHILE OTHERS FOLLOWED ANOTHER
HEZEKIAH • 729–687 — 2 KI 18–20		**722 TAKEN INTO ASSYRIAN CAPTIVITY**
	NAHUM / DANIEL / OBADIAH	
MANASSEH • 697–643 — 2 KI 21:1–18		
AMON • 643–641 — 2 KI 21:19–26		
JOSIAH • 641–609 — 2 KI 22–23:30	HABAKKUK / ZEPHANIAH / JEREMIAH / EZEKIEL	**586 TAKEN INTO BABYLONIAN CAPTIVITY**
JEHOAHAZ • 609–609 — 2 KI 23:31–35		
JEHOIAKIM • 609–598 — 2 KI 23:36–24:6		
JEHOIACHIN • 598–597 — 2 KI 24:8–17		
ZEDEKIAH • 597–586 — 2 KI 24:18–25:7		

CHAPTER TWELVE

SONGS

WISDOM

THE LONGING FOR
JESUS

In the middle of the Old Testament, between promises and prophecies and kings and battles, there is a surprising book that could appear to be an interruption to the ongoing story of Scripture. It's a songbook, a collection of 150 psalms that range from upbeat hymns of praise to mournful melodies of sorrow.

But make no mistake: the book of Psalms is more than the halftime show to the real action of the Old Testament. In fact, perhaps better than any other book, the Psalms capture the essence of the grand narrative of the Bible—God's covenantal relationship with his people.[1]

The people sing about the works of God, the character of God, the Word of God, and the promises of God. But even as they delight in God's ways, there is a voice of longing woven through each song. Though the people are enjoying some of the blessings of God, they know that the most precious promises of God are yet to be fulfilled. Even as they sing of what God has done, they also sing of what he is going to do—he will bring a Messiah, the Son of David, who will redeem the people and give them "a new song" to sing forever and ever (Revelation 5:9).

Longing for SALVATION

The psalms begin with a song about the promise of blessing for those who delight in God's Word rather than the delights of sin: "That person is like a tree planted by streams of water, which yields its fruit in season and whose leaf does not wither" (Psalm 1:3).

But even as the psalmist writes about the blessing of obedience, in another song, he acknowledges the inability of all mankind to obey God's law: "God looks down from heaven on all mankind to see if there are any who understand, any who seek God. Everyone has turned away, all have become corrupt; there is no one who does good, not even one" (Psalm 53:2–3). In light of their predicament, Israel longs for salvation from God: "Oh, that salvation for Israel would come out of Zion! When God restores his people, let Jacob rejoice and Israel be glad!" (Psalm 53:6).

The Longings of Israel

SALVATION

Oh, that salvation for Israel would come out of Zion! When God restores his people, let Jacob rejoice and Israel be glad! (Psalm 53:6)

REDEMPTION

"The Lord said to me, 'You are my Son; today I have begotten you. Ask of me, and I will make the nations your heritage and the ends of the earth your possession.'" (Psalm 2:7–8 ESV)

JUSTICE

Arise, LORD! Lift up your hand, O God. Do not forget the helpless. Why does the wicked man revile God? Why does he say to himself, "He won't call me to account"? (Psalm 10:12–13)

PURITY

Create in me a pure heart, O God, and renew a steadfast spirit within me . . . Restore to me the joy of your salvation and grant me a willing spirit, to sustain me. (Psalm 51:10, 12)

GOD'S PRESENCE

You make known to me the path of life; you will fill me with joy in your presence, with eternal pleasures at your right hand. (Psalm 16:11)

UNION

Place me like a seal over your heart, like a seal on your arm; for love is as strong as death, its jealousy unyielding as the grave. It burns like blazing fire, like a mighty flame. (Song of Songs 8:6)

WISDOM

The fear of the LORD is the beginning of knowledge. (Proverbs 1:7)

JESUS

- KING & SON • PSALM 2:8
- HE WHO WALKS BLAMELESSLY • PSALM 15
- THE ONE WHO MAKES OUR HEARTS CLEAN • PSALM 51
- THE ONE WHO WILL RESTORE THE JOY OF OUR SALVATION • PSALM 5
- ULTIMATE MANIFESTATION OF THE PRESENCE OF GOD • PSALM 16:11
- HE WHO DOES WHAT IS RIGHT • PSALM 15
- THE GOOD SHEPHERD • PSALM 23:3

Longing for
REDEMPTION

Through the promises given to King David, the people know that another King is coming, a King who will bring full redemption to Israel: "[The LORD] said to me, 'You are my son; today I have become your father. Ask me, and I will make the nations your inheritance, the ends of the earth your possession" (Psalm 2:7–8). Calling this King his "son," God recalls the promise of blessing given to Abraham and indicates that it will be fulfilled through the coming King, who is also the Son of the Lord (Psalm 110:1). This kingly Son will not only possess Israel, but all of the nations will be his inheritance.

Longing for
JUSTICE

The psalmist also repeatedly cries out to God for justice. In a world in which the wicked prosper and God's people are oppressed, he wonders why God does not take a stand and make all things right. "Arise, LORD! Lift up your hand, O God. Do not forget the helpless. Why does the wicked man revile God? Why does

he say to himself, 'He won't call me to account'?" (Psalm 10:12–13). In another psalm, Asaph laments the prosperity of the wicked: "This is what the wicked are like—always free of care, they go on amassing wealth. Surely in vain I have kept my heart pure and have washed my hands in innocence" (Psalm 73:12–13).

In every case of lamenting injustice, the psalmist looks forward to the day when God will right every wrong and carry out justice for the oppressed. "You, LORD, hear the desire of the afflicted; you encourage them, and you listen to their cry, defending the fatherless and the oppressed, so that mere earthly mortals will never again strike terror" (Psalm 10:17–18).

Longing for
PURITY

After committing adultery with a woman named Bathsheba and having her husband murdered, King David pens a song of repentance, which expresses his longing for purity and renewal.

First, he admits his fault before God: "I know my transgressions, and my sin is always before me. Against you, you only,

PSALMS

SUBJECT

# THANKSGIVING	# PRAISE
# PENITENTIAL	# HISTORICAL
# IMPRECATORY	# LAMENT
# ASCENTS	

ACROSTIC

✚ MESSIANIC

ASCRIBED TO

DAVID	D
ASAPH	A
KORAH	K
HEZEKIAH	H
ETHAN	E
SOLOMON	S
HEMAN	H
MOSES	M

BOOK 1

?	?	D	D	D	D	D	D	D	?	D	D	D	D	D	D	D	D	D	D	D	D
1	2	3	4	5	6	7	8	9	10	11	12	13	14	15	16	17	18	19	20	21	22

D	D	D	D	D	D	D	D	D	D	D	D	D	D	D	D	D	D	D
23	24	25	26	27	28	29	30	31	32	33	34	35	36	37	38	39	40	41

BOOK 2

K	K	K	K	K	K	K	K	K	A	D	D	D	D	D	D	D	D	D	D	D	D
42	43	44	45	46	47	48	49	50	51	52	53	54	55	56	57	58	59	60	61	62	63

D	D	?	?	D	D	D	?	D
64	65	66	67	68	69	70	71	72

BOOK 3

A	A	A	A	A	A	A	A	A	A	A	K	K	D	K	H	E
73	74	75	76	77	78	79	80	81	82	83	84	85	86	87	88	89

BOOK 4

M	?	?	?	?	?	?	?	?	?	?	D	?	D	?	D	?
90	91	92	93	94	95	96	97	98	99	100	101	102	103	104	105	106

BOOK 5

?	D	D	D	?	?	?	?	?	?	?	?	?	H	H	D	H	D	?	?	S	?
107	108	109	110	111	112	113	114	115	116	117	118	119	120	121	122	123	124	125	126	127	128

H	H	H	H	H	?	?		D	D	D	D	D	D	D	D	D	?	?	?	?
129	130	131	132	133	134	135	150	136	137	138	139	140	141	142	143	144	145	146	147	148	149

?
150

have I sinned and done what is evil in your sight" (Psalm 51:3–4). Knowing that he is stained with sin, he then asks God for purity: "Create in me a pure heart, O God, and renew a steadfast spirit within me . . . Restore to me the joy of your salvation and grant me a willing spirit" (Psalm 51:10, 12). Finally, he acknowledges that what he needs most is not a sacrificial offering, but a new heart: "You do not delight in sacrifice, or I would bring it; you do not take pleasure in burnt offerings. My sacrifice, O God, is a broken spirit; a broken and contrite heart you, God, will not despise" (Psalm 51:16–17).

In this psalm, David expresses a longing for purity that only God can provide. He knows that the sacrificial system cannot give him what he truly desires. He longs for a greater purity—one that goes all the way to the heart. In this, David looks forward to the purity to come through Jesus, the One who takes the bloodguiltiness from his people and gives them the purity of his own heart.

Longing for GOD'S PRESENCE

Even more than salvation or redemption or justice or purity, the psalmist longs for the presence of God. He expresses the universal heart cry of the people, a cry to be restored to the days before Adam's fall when man walked unashamed in God's presence. He expresses the unsurpassed joy of being with God: "You make known to me the path of life; you will fill me with joy in your presence, with eternal pleasures at your right hand" (Psalm 16:11). This is the supreme request of the psalmist: "One thing I ask from the LORD, this only do I seek: that I may dwell in the house of the LORD all the days of my life, to gaze on the beauty of the LORD and to seek him in his temple" (Psalm 27:4). And in the midst of trouble, the psalmist declares the only true hope for Israel: "God is our refuge and strength, an ever-present help in trouble . . . The LORD Almighty is with us; the God of Jacob is our fortress" (Psalm 46:1, 7).

Representing the entire nation of Israel, the psalmist expresses what they want most—the presence of God. Looking forward to the Messiah's future coming, the people long for the day when the sin of their hearts will be removed and once again they will walk with God unashamed.

Longing for UNION

In addition to the book of Psalms, Song of Songs is another extended poetic song within the canon of Scripture. This song is about a groom and his bride longing for sexual union in marriage, and the joys of that union when it is accomplished.

The song begins with the bride proclaiming, "Let him kiss me with the kisses of his mouth—for your love is more delightful than wine. Pleasing is the fragrance of your perfumes; your name is like perfume poured out" (Song of Songs 1:2–3). The bride is declaring that sexual union with her groom is more delightful than any earthly good or treasure. The husband returns his praise: "You are altogether beautiful, my darling; there is no flaw in you" (Song of Songs 4:7). Harking back to Adam's gaze at Eve, he is declaring the joy of being naked and unashamed in the purity of marriage.

At the end of this song, the bride makes a final request: "Set me as a seal upon your heart, as a seal upon your arm, for love is strong as death, jealousy is fierce as the grave. Its flashes are flashes of fire, the very flame of the LORD" (Song of Songs 8:6 ESV). In this request, the bride shows that while the song is primarily about the love between a husband and wife, it is also about the love of the Lord for his people. As the apostle Paul would later write, speaking of marriage, "This is a profound mystery—but I am talking about Christ and the church" (Ephesians 5:32).

Song of Songs speaks to the wonderful joy and blessing of God's intentions in marriage, even as it points us to a deeper longing for union with God and the pleasures that come from that union.[2]

THE COMPLEMENTARY UNION OF MARRIAGE
IMAGES A UNION WITH GOD

ATTRIBUTES
EMOTION • WILL • INTELLECT

CHARACTERISTICS
PROTECTOR • PROVIDER • PLANTER
NURTURER • CARETAKER • CULTIVATOR

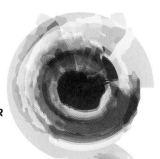

Then the LORD God formed a man from the dust of the ground . . .
Genesis 2:7

In the image of God he created them.
Genesis 1:27

MARRIAGE WAS CREATED FOR

COMPANIONSHIP
COOPERATION

The LORD God said, "It is not good for the man to be alone. I will make a helper suitable for him."
Genesis 2:18

. . . male and female he created them.
Genesis 1:27

PLEASURE
PROCREATION

God blessed them and said to them, "Be fruitful and increase in number; fill the earth and subdue it."
Genesis 1:28

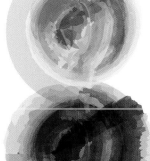

THE GLORY OF GOD
UNIFICATION

That is why a man leaves his father and mother and is united to his wife, and they become one flesh.
Genesis 2:24

A FORESHADOWING OF THE UNION OF CHRIST & THE CHURCH

This is a profound mystery—but I am talking about Christ and the church. However, each one of you also must love his wife as he loves himself, and the wife must respect her husband.
Ephesians 5:32–33

Longing for WISDOM

Along with the songs of the Bible, the books of Wisdom allow us to pause from the unfolding narrative so the readers of Scripture can reflect on their lives before the God of Israel. While the songs allow us to look upward to God from the reality of life, the books of Wisdom allow us to look inward to our lives from the reality of God.

As the Psalms begin with the blessed person who delights in the law of the Lord, the Proverbs begin with the wise person who walks in the fear of the Lord: "The fear of the LORD is the beginning of knowledge" (Proverbs 1:7). This is the foundation of Proverbs, indicating that we should see these sayings as instruction from a father to his son, teaching him how to walk wisely in the fear of the Lord.[3]

The book of Ecclesiastes brings us face-to-face with the "vanity" of life—the passing, temporal, and ultimately unfulfilling nature of the joys and pleasure of the created world. The Preacher, who is the son of David, tells us that he has gained all wisdom and wealth and riches and sex. And at the end of it all, he concludes, "Vanity of vanities . . . vanity of vanities! All is vanity" (Ecclesiastes 1:2 ESV). Having experienced all that can be experienced in life, he laments that he is still incomplete: "It is an unhappy business that God has given to the children of man to be busy with. I have seen everything that is done under the sun, and behold, all is vanity and a striving after wind" (Ecclesiastes 1:13–14 ESV). Because of life's meaninglessness, the Preacher instructs us not to set our hope on wealth (Ecclesiastes 5:10), not to set our hope on wisdom (Ecclesiastes 7:16), and not to set our hope on pleasure and achievement (Ecclesiastes 2:11). Instead, we ought to fear the Lord and enjoy the gifts that he provides.

The book of Job is a vivid portrait of the harshness of life that Ecclesiastes describes. It tells the story of a godly man, Job, who is placed under severe suffering, including the loss of his possessions, his family, and his health. Though he cannot see the underlying reasons for his suffering, we as readers are able to see that Satan is tempting Job, testing him with God's permission. While Job begins his suffering with praise to God (Job 1:20–22),

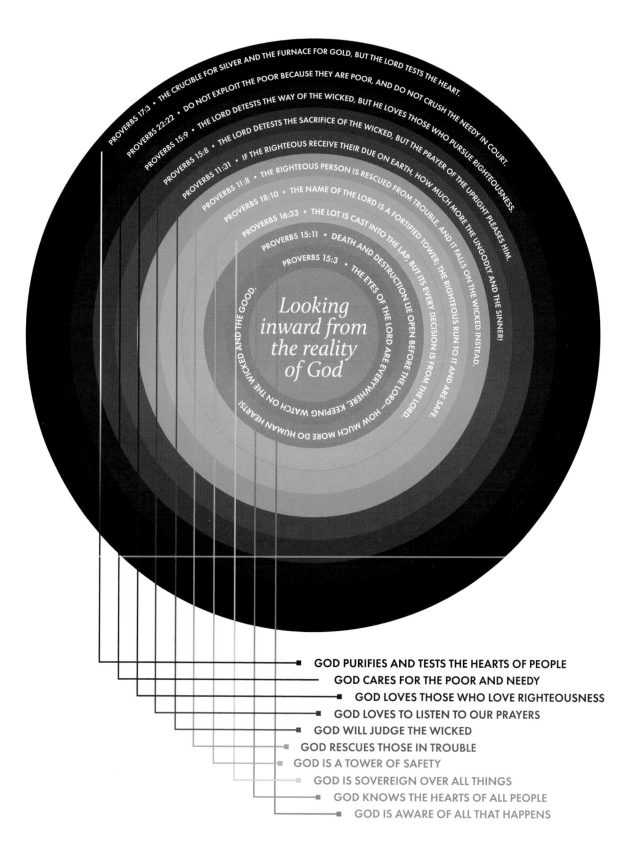

PROVERBS 17:3 • THE CRUCIBLE FOR SILVER AND THE FURNACE FOR GOLD, BUT THE LORD TESTS THE HEART.

PROVERBS 22:22 • DO NOT EXPLOIT THE POOR BECAUSE THEY ARE POOR, AND DO NOT CRUSH THE NEEDY IN COURT.

PROVERBS 15:9 • THE LORD DETESTS THE WAY OF THE WICKED, BUT HE LOVES THOSE WHO PURSUE RIGHTEOUSNESS.

PROVERBS 15:8 • THE LORD DETESTS THE SACRIFICE OF THE WICKED, BUT THE PRAYER OF THE UPRIGHT PLEASES HIM.

PROVERBS 11:31 • IF THE RIGHTEOUS RECEIVE THEIR DUE ON EARTH, HOW MUCH MORE THE UNGODLY AND THE SINNER!

PROVERBS 11:8 • THE RIGHTEOUS PERSON IS RESCUED FROM TROUBLE, AND IT FALLS ON THE WICKED INSTEAD.

PROVERBS 18:10 • THE NAME OF THE LORD IS A FORTIFIED TOWER, THE RIGHTEOUS RUN TO IT AND ARE SAFE.

PROVERBS 16:33 • THE LOT IS CAST INTO THE LAP, BUT ITS EVERY DECISION IS FROM THE LORD.

PROVERBS 15:11 • DEATH AND DESTRUCTION LIE OPEN BEFORE THE LORD— HOW MUCH MORE DO HUMAN HEARTS!

PROVERBS 15:3 • THE EYES OF THE LORD ARE EVERYWHERE, KEEPING WATCH ON THE WICKED AND THE GOOD.

Looking inward from the reality of God

GOD PURIFIES AND TESTS THE HEARTS OF PEOPLE

GOD CARES FOR THE POOR AND NEEDY

GOD LOVES THOSE WHO LOVE RIGHTEOUSNESS

GOD LOVES TO LISTEN TO OUR PRAYERS

GOD WILL JUDGE THE WICKED

GOD RESCUES THOSE IN TROUBLE

GOD IS A TOWER OF SAFETY

GOD IS SOVEREIGN OVER ALL THINGS

GOD KNOWS THE HEARTS OF ALL PEOPLE

GOD IS AWARE OF ALL THAT HAPPENS

he later wavers between complaint and hope (Job 13:15; 19:25–27), asking God to reveal himself. At the very end of the book, the Lord does arrive, and he challenges Job: "Brace yourself like a man; I will question you, and you shall answer me . . . Do you have an arm like God's, and can your voice thunder like his?" (Job 40:7, 9). After encountering God, Job responds with repentance and praise: "My ears had heard of you but now my eyes have seen you. Therefore I despise myself and repent in dust and ashes" (Job 42:5–6). The book of Job shows us that even when we do not understand the reasons for our suffering, God is still in control. This encourages us to walk in the fear of the Lord, even in the midst of our suffering: "The fear of the Lord—that is wisdom, and to shun evil is understanding" (Job 28:28).

Longing for JESUS

The songs within Psalms and Song of Songs ultimately express a longing for Jesus. He is the King and the Son who will have the nations as his inheritance and the ends of the earth as his possession (Psalm 2:8). He fulfills the portrait of the righteous person in Psalm 15:2–3: "the one whose walk is blameless, who does what is righteous, who speaks the truth from their heart; whose tongue utters no slander, who does no wrong to a neighbor, and cast no slur on others." He is the ultimate manifestation of the presence of God, in whom we have fullness of joy and at whose right hand we have eternal pleasures (Psalm 16:11). He is the one who was "poured out like water," whose hands and feet were pierced, whose garments were divided, and who will be praised to the coming generations (Psalm 22:14, 16, 18, 30–31). He is the good Shepherd who leads us along the right paths for the glory of God (Psalm 23:3). He is the one who can make our hearts pure and restore the joy of our salvation (Psalm 51:10–12). And he is the one to whom the Lord said, "Sit at my right hand until I make your enemies a footstool for your feet" (Psalm 110:1).

From the first note to the last, a longing for Jesus is the theme of every song of Scripture.

MESSIANIC PROPHECIES IN THE PSALMS ✚ ━━━━━━━━━━ ✚ NT FULFILLMENT

PSALM 16:10	HIS RESURRECTION	ACTS 13:35
PSALM 22:1, 6-8, 18; 31:5; 34:20; 69:21	HIS SUFFERINGS	JOHN 19:33–36
PSALM 24:7–8	HIS TRIUMPHAL ENTRY INTO GLORY	PHILIPPIANS 2:9–11
PSALM 40:6–10	HIS OBEDIENCE	HEBREWS 10:5–7
PSALM 41:9; 55:12–14	HIS BETRAYAL	MATTHEW 26:14–16
PSALM 45:2, 6, 8, 13, 15	HIS MARRIAGE TO THE CHURCH	REVELATION 19:7–10
PSALM 68:18	HIS ASCENSION	EPHESIANS 4:8
PSALM 69:9	HIS ZEAL	JOHN 2:17
PSALM 72:17; 89:27; 102:16–21	HIS MILLENNIAL REIGN	REVELATION 11:15
PSALM 109:2-3	HIS FALSE WITNESSES	MATTHEW 26:59–61
PSALM 109:4	HIS PRAYER FOR HIS ENEMIES	LUKE 23:34
PSALM 110:1, 6	HIS DESTRUCTION OF THE HEATHEN	REVELATION 6–19
PSALM 110:4	HIS HIGH PRIESTLY WORK	HEBREWS 5–7
PSALM 118:22	HIS REJECTION	MATTHEW 21:42

Like the songs, the Bible's books of Wisdom also point us forward to a longing for Jesus. In Proverbs, we see a picture of Jesus, the Son of God, who perfectly feared the Lord, turned away from evil, and walked in wisdom all of his days. In Ecclesiastes, we are challenged to acknowledge the vanity of earthly life—the truth that our longings will not be satisfied in this world—and to refocus our longing on Jesus, who will bring a new heaven and a new earth that endures forever. And in Job, we find a longing for a Mediator, one who will stand between us and God—Jesus Christ, who will defend us from the accusations of our accuser, the devil, and one who suffered perfectly on our behalf in the fear of the Lord.

CHAPTER THIRTEEN

PROPHETS

EXILE

NEW COVENANT

EXPECTATION OF

JESUS

As we have seen, the story of Jesus does not begin with the first chapter of the New Testament. Hundreds of years before Jesus was born, his arrival was promised and longed for. Jesus is the promised child of Eve who will crush the head of the serpent. He is the promised offspring of Abraham through whom God will bless all the nations. And he is the promised heir of David's throne whose kingdom will never end.

Even with these precious promises, Israel takes a turn for the worse. Their temple is destroyed, and they are sent into exile. Because of their persistent disobedience and idolatry, they are removed from the land, just as God had promised. The light of God's people, intended to enlighten the nations, seems to be dimming. But even in the darkness of exile, there are some bright promises of hope: God will rebuild his fallen temple, and a Suffering Servant is coming who will take away their sin.

EXPECTING THE SUFFERING SERVANT

The prophet Isaiah wrote after the reign of King Uzziah and nearly eight hundred years before the arrival of Jesus. At this time, God's people were divided into the northern kingdom of Israel and the southern kingdom of Judah. In the midst of the wickedness of the people, God gave Isaiah a glorious vision of the heavenly throne room and called him to minister to the hard-hearted people of Israel: "Go and tell this people: 'Be ever hearing, but never understanding; be ever seeing, but never perceiving" (Isaiah 6:9). God was about to reveal wonderful truth through Isaiah, but the people were not going to receive it.

Early in his book, Isaiah tells of a coming Messiah: "The people walking in darkness have seen a great light . . . For to us a child is born, to us a son is given, and the government will be on his shoulders. And he will be called Wonderful Counselor, Mighty God, Everlasting Father, Prince of Peace" (Isaiah 9:2, 6). According to Isaiah, there would be a light to shine into the darkness of Israel; a child will be born, and he will be called "Mighty God" and "Everlasting Father."

A couple of chapters later, Isaiah recalls the promise given to King David, the son of Jesse: "A shoot will come up from the stump of Jesse; from his roots a Branch will bear fruit. The Spirit of the LORD will

A PICTURE OF THE PROMISED RESCUER FROM ISAIAH

BORN OF A VIRGIN

ISAIAH 7:14

CALLED IMMANUEL GOD WITH US

HE WILL BE A HUMAN CHILD

ISAIAH 9:6

HE WILL BE A LIGHT TO THE GENTILES

HE WILL RESTORE ISRAEL

ISAIAH 49:6

HIS PEOPLE WILL NOT BELIEVE IN HIM

ISAIAH 53:1

HE WILL BE DESPISED & REJECTED

ISAIAH 53:3

HE WILL BE EXALTED BY GOD

ISAIAH 53:12

AFTER HIS SUFFERINGS THE FATHER WILL BE SATISFIED

BECAUSE OF HIS SUFFERINGS HE WILL JUSTIFY HIS PEOPLE

ISAIAH 53:11

HE WILL
BE GOD

NAMED
WONDERFUL
COUNSELOR
MIGHTY GOD
EVERLASTING FATHER
PRINCE OF PEACE

HE WILL
SIT ON
THE
THRONE
OF DAVID

ISAIAH 9:7

THERE
WILL BE
NO END
TO HIS
GOVERNMENT

HE WILL
RULE WITH
JUSTICE &
RIGHTEOUSNESS

BIRTH

MINISTRY   FUTURE

DEATH

HE WILL
SUFFER
GREATLY

ISAIAH 53:4

HE WILL
BE PIERCED
AND CRUSHED
FOR HIS
PEOPLE

ISAIAH 53:5

HIS FATHER
WILLED HIS
SUFFERING &
ALL THAT
WOULD
HAPPEN

ISAIAH 53:10

WE
WILL STILL
TURN OUR
BACKS ON
HIM

ISAIAH 53:6

HIS WOUNDS
WILL
HEAL US
& BRING
PEACE

rest on him—the Spirit of wisdom and of understanding, the Spirit of counsel and of might, the Spirit of the knowledge and fear of the LORD" (Isaiah 11:1–2). Although Israel may have wondered if God's promise to keep David's descendant on the throne forever had been forgotten, Isaiah says that one of David's descendants will indeed take the throne again. Like David, this promised "Branch" of David will be filled with the Spirit and will lead the people in the fear of the Lord.

Toward the end of his writings, Isaiah writes of a Suffering Servant: "See, my servant will act wisely; he will be raised and lifted up and highly exalted" (Isaiah 52:13). Isaiah then relates in detail what the Servant does for the people of God: "Surely he took up our pain and bore our suffering, yet we considered him punished by God, stricken by him, and afflicted. But he was pierced for our transgressions, he was crushed for our iniquities; the punishment that brought us peace was on him, and by his wounds we are healed. We all, like sheep, have gone astray; each of us has turned to our own way; and the LORD has laid on him the iniquity of us all" (Isaiah 53:4–6). Isaiah foretells that the Suffering Servant will be lifted high,

but he will also be crushed; he will be exalted, but he will also carry our iniquity and sin; he will be wounded, but it is by his wounds that we will be healed.

Isaiah brings three bright rays of hope to Israel: a coming Child, a coming King, and a coming Servant. Few would have guessed that these promises would one day be fulfilled in a single man, Jesus Christ. What Isaiah foreshadows in the Old Testament, Jesus fulfills in the New Testament. Jesus is the Child on whose shoulders God places the government and rule of this world, the one who is both human and "Mighty God." Jesus is the promised King, the "Branch" or descendant of David, who is filled with the Spirit, reigning and judging with wisdom. And Jesus is the Suffering Servant who is crushed for our iniquities, paying the just penalty for the sins of God's people. His wounds are what bring us peace with God and healing from the curse of sin.

EXPECTING A NEW COVENANT

As Israel is sent into exile from the land and the temple is destroyed, they have the promise of the coming Messiah, a King who will reign over them in justice, and a Suffering Servant who will take away

BIBLICAL COVENANTS

NOAH
GENESIS 9:8–17

God promised never to destroy the earth again with a worldwide flood in the unconditional convenant, signed with a rainbow as a promise.

ABRAHAM
GENESIS 12:7; 13:14–17; 15:6; 16–18

In a vision, God promised unconditionally to make Abraham a great nation, bless and curse those who do the same to him, and bless all peoples of the earth through him.

NEW IN JESUS
JEREMIAH 31:27–40

God promised with no conditions to give Israel a new heart to obey him, to dwell in the land forever, and to always enjoy the presence of God.

MOSES
EXODUS 19:3–8

God promised to bless and care for the people of Israel if they obeyed him completely. If they did not obey, God would curse them.

DAVID
2 SAMUEL 7:11–16

God promised David unconditionally that his reign and throne would last forever.

their sins. But how will this King reign over them, and how will he take away their sins?

Ever since the law was given to Moses, the people demonstrated an utter inability to obey God and receive life through the law. If their future relationship with God was to be based on their ongoing obedience to the law, they were still in a hopeless position. Unless something changed, the cycle of sin and judgment would keep repeating itself.

Aware of their need, God raises up more prophets to tell of a coming day when he will establish a new covenant with his people. While the old covenant failed and did not endure, the new covenant will be everlasting.

Writing at the beginning of the exile, Jeremiah reminds the people of their disobedience to God: "My people have exchanged their glorious God for worthless idols . . . My people have committed two sins: They have forsaken me, the spring of living water, and have dug their own cisterns, broken cisterns that cannot hold water" (Jeremiah 2:11, 13). The people had forsaken God and trusted in worthless idols that could do nothing for them.

After several chapters of pronouncing judgment on the people, Jeremiah confirms Isaiah's promise of the coming Davidic King: "'The days are coming,' declares the LORD, 'when I will raise up for David a righteous Branch, a King who will reign wisely and do what is just and right in the land'" (Jeremiah 23:5). Just as God had promised to David, he will one day bring a righteous descendant to take up the throne.

Later, Jeremiah provides stunning clarity about how God will deal with his people under the reign of this coming King: "'The days are coming,' declares the LORD, 'when I will make a new covenant with the people of Israel and with the people of Judah. It will not be like the covenant I made with their ancestors when I took them by the hand to lead them out of Egypt, because they broke my covenant, though I was a husband to them,' declares the LORD . . . 'I will put my law in their minds and write it on their hearts. I will be their God, and they will be my people . . . For I will forgive their wickedness and will remember their sins no more'" (Jeremiah 31:31–34).

THE NEW COVENANT IN JEREMIAH 31:31–34, ESV

The Messianic Era, the time of Jesus

GOD WILL UNIFY THE SPLIT KINGDOM

The old covenant was conditional, resulting in judgment; this new covenant is unconditional, resulting in blessing

"Behold, the days are coming, declares the LORD, when I will make a new covenant with the house of Israel and the house of Judah, not like the covenant that I made with their fathers on the day when I took them by the hand to bring them out of the land of Egypt, my covenant that they broke, though I was their husband, declares the LORD. For this is the covenant that I will make with the house of Israel after those days, declares the LORD: I will put my law within them, and I will write it on their hearts. And I will be their God, and they shall be my people. And no longer shall each one teach his neighbor and each his brother, saying, 'Know the LORD,' for they shall all know me, from the least of them to the greatest, declares the LORD. For I will forgive their iniquity, and I will remember their sin no more."

They could not keep the Mosaic Covenant, no matter how hard they tried

GOD WAS THE FAITHFUL SPOUSE

True knowledge of the LORD will be shared by all

NOT WRITTEN ON TABLETS OF STONE EXTERNALLY, BUT ON THE INSIDE, WHICH WILL RESULT IN REAL CHANGE

THEY WILL NOW HAVE THE ABILITY TO OBEY FOREVER.

Sin will no longer result in curses and separation but will be completely paid for by the blood of Jesus

100 REFERENCES, PROPHECIES, & FULFILLMENTS

The life of Jesus is woven throughout the Scriptures

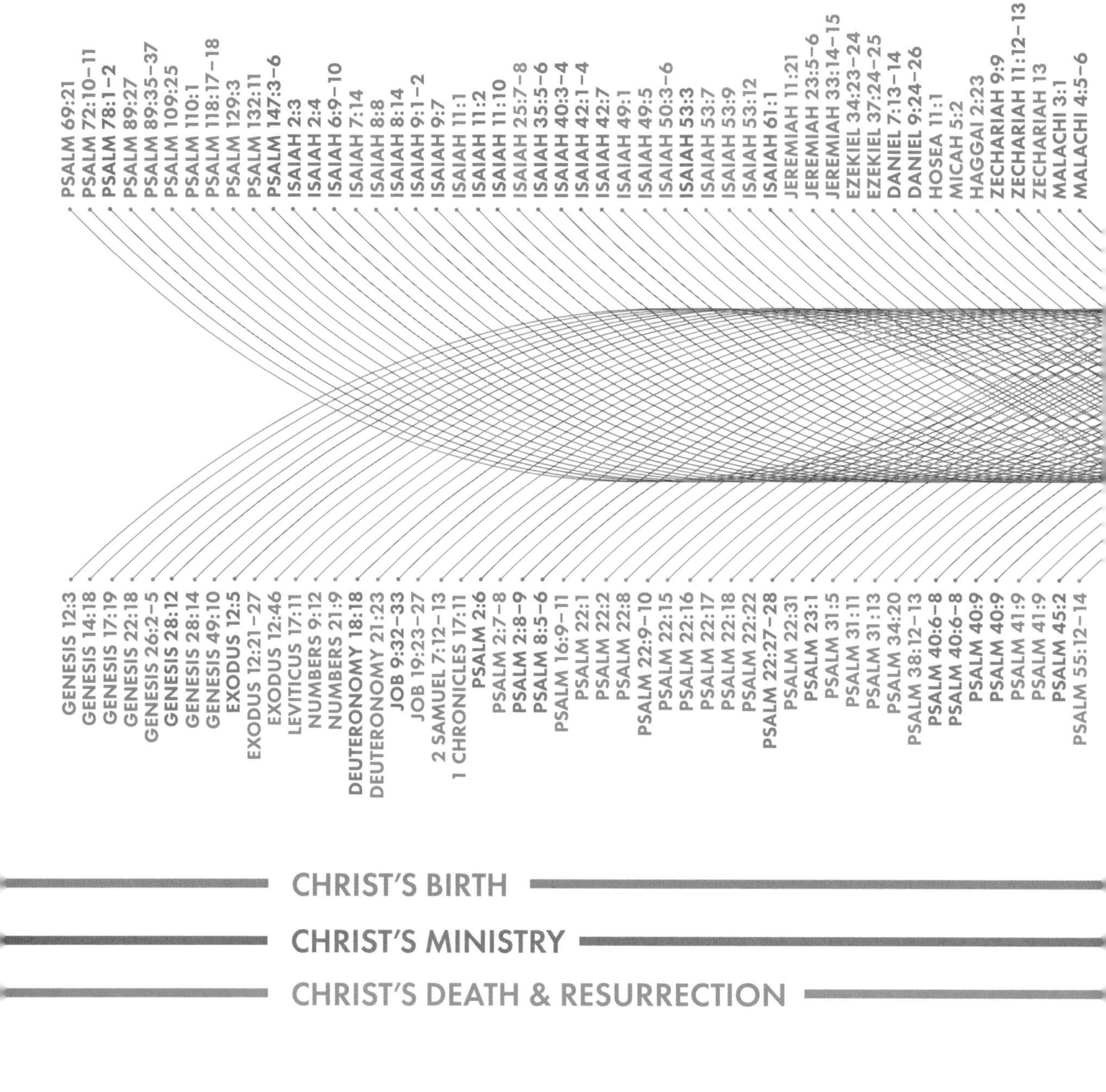

Top references (left to right):

PSALM 69:21 · PSALM 72:10–11 · PSALM 78:1–2 · PSALM 89:27 · PSALM 89:35–37 · PSALM 109:25 · PSALM 110:1 · PSALM 118:17–18 · PSALM 129:3 · PSALM 132:11 · PSALM 147:3–6 · ISAIAH 2:3 · ISAIAH 2:4 · ISAIAH 6:9–10 · ISAIAH 7:14 · ISAIAH 8:8 · ISAIAH 8:14 · ISAIAH 9:1–2 · ISAIAH 9:7 · ISAIAH 11:1 · ISAIAH 11:2 · ISAIAH 11:10 · ISAIAH 25:7–8 · ISAIAH 35:5–6 · ISAIAH 40:3–4 · ISAIAH 42:1–4 · ISAIAH 42:7 · ISAIAH 49:1 · ISAIAH 49:5 · ISAIAH 50:3–6 · ISAIAH 53:3 · ISAIAH 53:7 · ISAIAH 53:9 · ISAIAH 53:12 · ISAIAH 61:1 · JEREMIAH 11:21 · JEREMIAH 23:5–6 · JEREMIAH 33:14–15 · EZEKIEL 34:23–24 · EZEKIEL 37:24–25 · DANIEL 7:13–14 · DANIEL 9:24–26 · HOSEA 11:1 · MICAH 5:2 · HAGGAI 2:23 · ZECHARIAH 9:9 · ZECHARIAH 11:12–13 · ZECHARIAH 13 · MALACHI 3:1 · MALACHI 4:5–6

Bottom references (left to right):

GENESIS 12:3 · GENESIS 14:18 · GENESIS 17:19 · GENESIS 22:18 · GENESIS 26:2–5 · GENESIS 28:12 · GENESIS 28:14 · GENESIS 49:10 · EXODUS 12:5 · EXODUS 12:21–27 · EXODUS 12:46 · LEVITICUS 17:11 · NUMBERS 9:12 · NUMBERS 21:9 · DEUTERONOMY 18:18 · DEUTERONOMY 21:23 · JOB 9:32–33 · JOB 19:23–27 · 2 SAMUEL 7:12–13 · 1 CHRONICLES 17:11 · PSALM 2:6 · PSALM 2:7–8 · PSALM 2:8–9 · PSALM 8:5–6 · PSALM 16:9–11 · PSALM 22:1 · PSALM 22:2 · PSALM 22:8 · PSALM 22:9–10 · PSALM 22:15 · PSALM 22:16 · PSALM 22:17 · PSALM 22:18 · PSALM 22:22 · PSALM 22:27–28 · PSALM 22:31 · PSALM 23:1 · PSALM 31:5 · PSALM 31:11 · PSALM 31:13 · PSALM 34:20 · PSALM 38:12–13 · PSALM 40:6–8 · PSALM 40:6–8 · PSALM 40:9 · PSALM 40:9 · PSALM 41:9 · PSALM 45:2 · PSALM 55:12–14

Legend:

CHRIST'S BIRTH

CHRIST'S MINISTRY

CHRIST'S DEATH & RESURRECTION

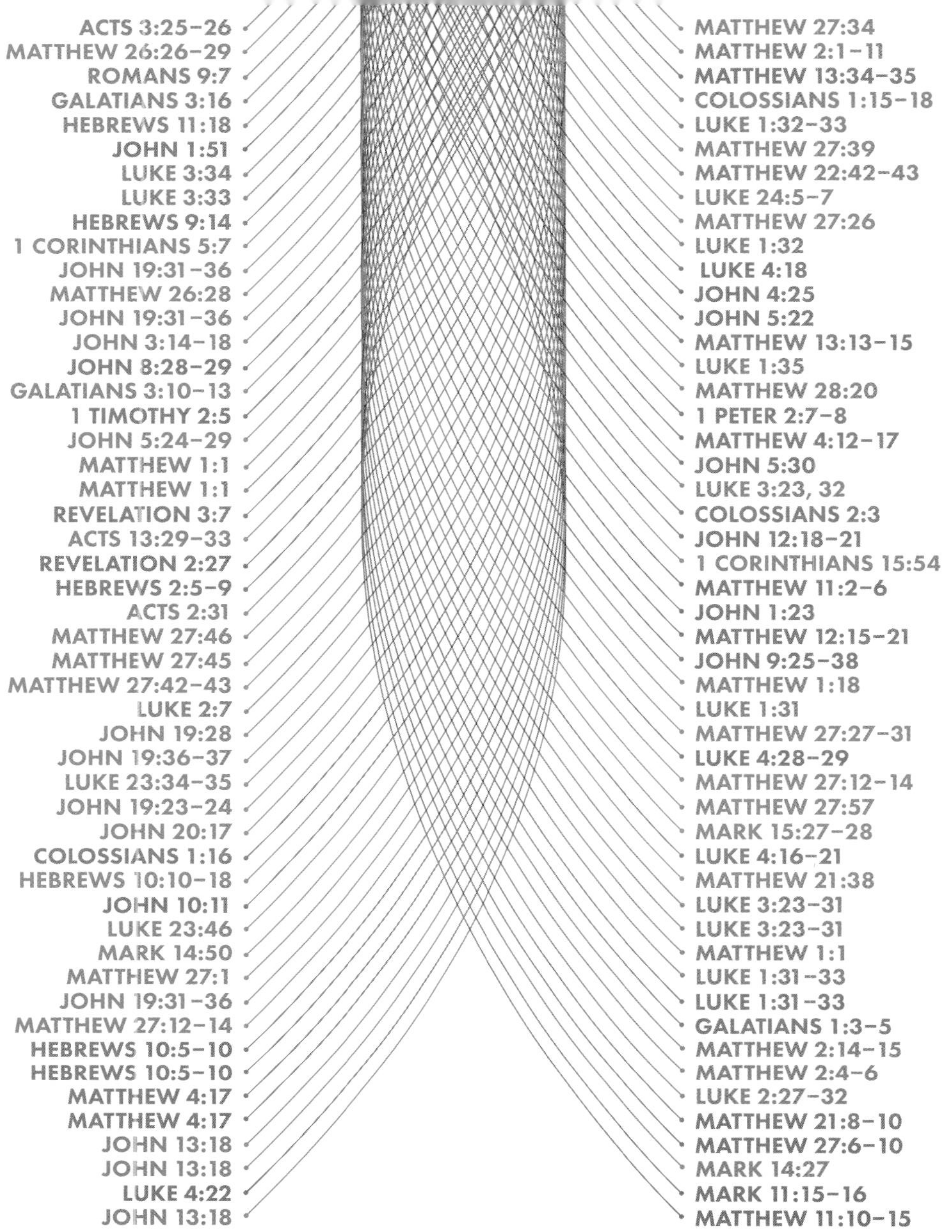

Top labels (left to right):

MATTHEW 27:34
MATTHEW 2:1–11
MATTHEW 13:34–35
COLOSSIANS 1:15–18
LUKE 1:32–33
MATTHEW 27:39
MATTHEW 22:42–43
LUKE 24:5–7
MATTHEW 27:26
LUKE 1:32
LUKE 4:18
JOHN 4:25
JOHN 5:22
MATTHEW 13:13–15
LUKE 1:35
MATTHEW 28:20
1 PETER 2:7–8
MATTHEW 4:12–17
JOHN 5:30
LUKE 3:23, 32
COLOSSIANS 2:3
JOHN 12:18–21
1 CORINTHIANS 15:54
MATTHEW 11:2–6
JOHN 1:23
MATTHEW 12:15–21
JOHN 9:25–38
MATTHEW 1:18
LUKE 1:31
MATTHEW 27:27–31
LUKE 4:28–29
MATTHEW 27:12–14
MATTHEW 27:57
MARK 15:27–28
LUKE 4:16–21
MATTHEW 21:38
LUKE 3:23–31
LUKE 3:23–31
MATTHEW 1:1
LUKE 1:31–33
LUKE 1:31–33
GALATIANS 1:3–5
MATTHEW 2:14–15
MATTHEW 2:4–6
LUKE 2:27–32
MATTHEW 21:8–10
MATTHEW 27:6–10
MARK 14:27
MARK 11:15–16
MATTHEW 11:10–15

Bottom labels (left to right):

ACTS 3:25–26
MATTHEW 26:26–29
ROMANS 9:7
GALATIANS 3:16
HEBREWS 11:18
JOHN 1:51
LUKE 3:34
LUKE 3:33
HEBREWS 9:14
1 CORINTHIANS 5:7
JOHN 19:31–36
MATTHEW 26:28
JOHN 19:31–36
JOHN 3:14–18
JOHN 8:28–29
GALATIANS 3:10–13
1 TIMOTHY 2:5
JOHN 5:24–29
MATTHEW 1:1
MATTHEW 1:1
REVELATION 3:7
ACTS 13:29–33
REVELATION 2:27
HEBREWS 2:5–9
ACTS 2:31
MATTHEW 27:46
MATTHEW 27:45
MATTHEW 27:42–43
LUKE 2:7
JOHN 19:28
JOHN 19:36–37
LUKE 23:34–35
JOHN 19:23–24
JOHN 20:17
COLOSSIANS 1:16
HEBREWS 10:10–18
JOHN 10:11
LUKE 23:46
MARK 14:50
MATTHEW 27:1
JOHN 19:31–36
HEBREWS 10:5–10
HEBREWS 10:5–10
MATTHEW 4:17
MATTHEW 4:17
JOHN 13:18
JOHN 13:18
LUKE 4:22
JOHN 13:18

Jeremiah says that the new covenant will be unlike the old covenant, which was broken and failed to produce life. Instead of giving the people the law on tablets of stone, God will now write the law on their hearts—just as he intended all along. He will forgive the iniquities of the people, and he will not remember their sins.

The prophet Ezekiel, writing around the same time, gives a similar promise to the people: "I will sprinkle clean water on you, and you will be clean; I will cleanse you from all your impurities and from all your idols. I will give you a new heart and put a new spirit in you; I will remove from you your heart of stone and give you a heart of flesh. And I will put my Spirit in you and move you to follow my decrees and be careful to keep my laws. Then you will live in the land I gave your ancestors; you will be my people, and I will be your God" (Ezekiel 36:25–28).

God now promises to put his Spirit in his people and to cause them to walk in his statutes and obey his rules. How? He is going to give them a new heart and a new spirit that enables them to walk in obedience.

In the midst of the Israelites' exile, the prophet Daniel confirms the promise given to David and speaks of a coming "son of man": "He was given authority, glory and sovereign power; all nations and peoples of every language worshiped him" (Daniel 7:14). Again, we are reminded of the promised King, the one who will rule on God's throne over all the nations of the earth.

As we near the final pages of the Old Testament, we find a rich and beautiful thread of promises, which woven together create a tapestry of expectation: out of the darkness of exile and the failure of the old covenant, God is sending a Righteous King, a Suffering Servant, the Promised Offspring, the Son of Man, and through him God will establish a new, everlasting covenant with his people in which he will be their God and his Spirit will dwell in them.

Before the bright light of Jesus arrives on the scene, the last prophet Malachi speaks of his forerunner: "I will send my messenger, who will prepare the way before me" (Malachi 3:1). Soon, the way for Adam's fallen descendants to return to their Creator will be prepared; the promises made to Abraham will reach fulfillment; and the coming Davidic King, the one spoken of by the prophets, will finally step into history.

JESUS
IS GREATER THAN

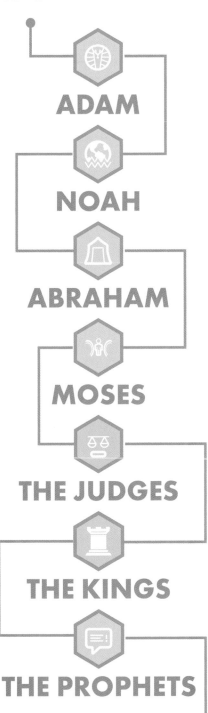

ADAM

NOAH

ABRAHAM

MOSES

THE JUDGES

THE KINGS

THE PROPHETS

CHAPTER FOURTEEN

GOSPEL

KINGDOM

THE COMING OF
JESUS

In the very first pages of the New Testament, the promised Son of David, the long-expected King of Israel, and the hoped-for Savior of the world arrives.

By connecting Jesus Christ with Abraham and David in a long genealogy at the beginning of the first gospel, Matthew makes it clear that Jesus is the ultimate fulfillment of the promises made to Abraham and to David. He is the one through whom the nations will be blessed. He is the one whose throne will endure forever. And just as God chose weak people to accomplish his purposes in the Old Testament, the New Testament begins with God doing the same.

THE LIFE OF JESUS

There are four accounts of Jesus' life, each written by a different person and presenting a different perspective on his life and death. In Matthew, Mark, Luke, and John, commonly called "the gospels," we have a detailed look at the life of Jesus Christ and the message he came to proclaim.

Jesus' story begins with what appears to be a scandal. Mary, a virgin betrothed to a man named Joseph, is visited by an angel from the Lord and told that she will conceive a son through the Holy Spirit, and this child will be the promised Son of God and King of Israel: "The Lord God will give him the throne of his father David, and he will reign over Jacob's descendants forever; his kingdom will never end" (Luke 1:32–33).

Seeing Mary's pregnancy, Joseph assumes she has committed adultery. But being a good man, he tries to divorce her quietly without shaming her. But the same angel appears to Joseph and repeats the promise given to Mary: "Do not be afraid to take Mary home as your wife, because what is conceived in her is from the Holy Spirit. She will give birth to a son, and you are to give him the name Jesus, because he will save his people from their sins" (Matthew 1:20–21).

Both Jesus' divinity and royalty are made clear from his birth. An army of angels appears and shout their praises to God, and wise men from far-off lands travel to visit him. They fall down in worship and bear gifts representing the nations' treasures. As a young boy, Jesus displays unsurpassed wisdom and understanding, and year by year, he "grew in wisdom and stature, and in favor with God and man" (Luke 2:52).

THE CHILD OF PROMISE

♛ MATTHEW
JESUS THE KING

Matthew traces the lineage of Jesus from Abraham to Joseph. Writing to a Jewish audience, Matthew apparently intends to establish that Jesus is the heir to David's throne and is worthy to inherit the kingdom. His list includes two sections of 14 names and one of 12 names.

👤 LUKE
JESUS THE GOD-MAN

Luke traces the lineage of Jesus from Adam to Joseph. Writing to a Greek audience, Luke apparently intends to establish the humanity of Jesus by showing that he descended from God through Adam and is thus a Savior for all of humanity. His list includes 77 names.

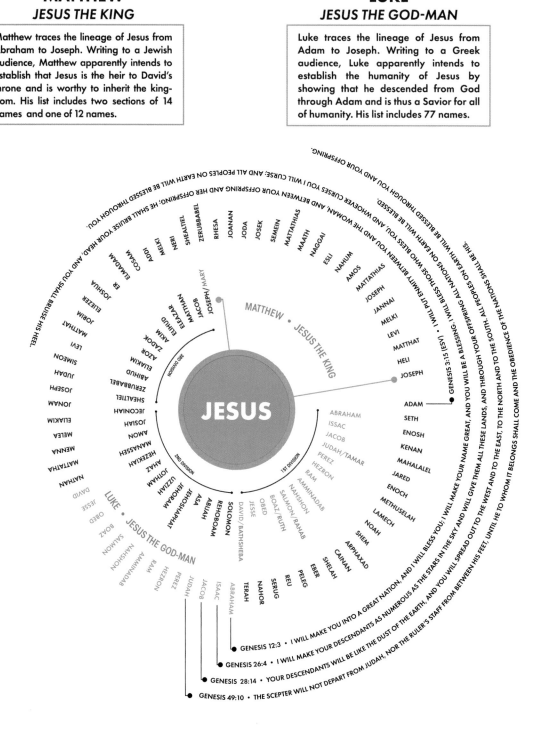

John the Baptist, a cousin of Jesus, prepares the way for the Lord, fulfilling the final prophecy of the prophet Malachi. He calls the crowds to turn from their sin and proclaims a baptism of repentance, turning away from their sin and back to the ways of God. In the midst of John's preaching ministry, Jesus, now an adult, inaugurates his ministry by being baptized by John. This baptism identifies Jesus with Israel and their sins, yet even in his baptism, God makes it known that Jesus is set apart from every other person, proclaiming: "You are my Son, whom I love; with you I am well pleased" (Luke 3:22).

Before beginning his ministry, Jesus is led by the Spirit of God into the wilderness, where he fasts for forty days. At the end of the forty days, he is tempted by Satan three times. Each time, he rebukes Satan with the Word of God and proves his obedience. While Israel gave in to temptation during their forty years in the wilderness, Jesus fends off every temptation during his forty days in the desert. While Adam and Eve listened to the lies of Satan and disobeyed God, Jesus proclaims the truth to Satan and obeys God. In every place where God's people failed, the Son of God was faithful.

Knowing that his days on earth would be short, Jesus calls twelve disciples to himself, "that they might be with him and that he might send them out to preach and to have authority to drive out demons" (Mark 3:14–15). These men would walk with Jesus and observe everything that he did and said, and after he left the world, they would be empowered by the Holy Spirit to carry on his work.

The predominant message proclaimed by Jesus throughout his ministry is well summarized by Mark: "The time has come . . . The kingdom of God has come near. Repent and believe the good news" (Mark 1:15). Jesus was declaring that with his coming, the kingdom of God—the longed-for rule and reign of God—had finally come. And with the coming of the kingdom, the people must turn from their sins and believe in the gospel.

ISAIAH 53:7

He was oppressed and afflicted, yet he did not open his mouth; he was led like a lamb to the slaughter . . .

EXODUS 29:38–39

This is what you are to offer on the altar regularly each day: two lambs a year old. Offer one in the morning and the other at twilight.

ISAIAH 53:10

Yet it was the LORD's will to crush him and cause him to suffer, and though the LORD makes his life an offering for sin . . .

EXODUS 12:3, 7, 13

Each man is to take a lamb . . . they are to take some of the blood and put it on the sides and tops of the doorframes of the houses where they eat the lambs . . . The blood will be a sign for you on the houses where you are, and when I see the blood, I will pass over you.

LOOK! THE LAMB OF GOD, WHO TAKES AWAY THE SIN OF THE WORLD!

JOHN 1:29

HEBREWS 10:1-4

The law is only a shadow of the good things that are coming—not the realities themselves. For this reason it can never, by the same sacrifices repeated endlessly year after year, make perfect those who draw near to worship. Otherwise, would they not have stopped being offered? For the worshipers would have been cleansed once for all, and would no longer have felt guilty for their sins. But those sacrifices are an annual reminder of sins.

IT IS IMPOSSIBLE FOR THE BLOOD OF BULLS AND GOATS TO TAKE AWAY SINS.

JOHN 1:34

I have seen and I testify that this is God's Chosen One.

HEBREWS 10:8-10

First he said, "Sacrifices and offerings, burnt offerings and sin offerings you did not desire, nor were you pleased with them"—though they were offered in accordance with the law. Then he said, "Here I am, I have come to do your will." He sets aside the first to establish the second.

ROMANS 8:3

For what the law was powerless to do because it was weakened by the flesh, God did by sending his own Son in the likeness of sinful flesh to be a sin offering.

AND BY THAT WILL, WE HAVE BEEN MADE HOLY THROUGH THE SACRIFICE OF THE BODY OF JESUS CHRIST ONCE FOR ALL.

With countless miracles, Jesus demonstrated that he was inaugurating the kingdom of God. He turned water into wine, walked on water, healed the sick, raised the dead, and multiplied bread and fish to feed thousands. These miracles weren't meant to merely draw crowds or create a stir. They were meant to give the people a foretaste of the kingdom of God, a picture of how God in Jesus Christ was going to reverse the effects of sin. When John the Baptist sent his disciples to ask whether Jesus was the promised Messiah, Jesus replied, "Go back and report to John what you hear and see: The blind receive sight, the lame walk, those who have leprosy are cleansed, the deaf hear, the dead are raised, and the good news is proclaimed to the poor. Blessed is anyone who does not stumble on account of me" (Matthew 11:4–6). In each miracle, Jesus showed that he was indeed the Promised One to come.[1]

With his teachings, Jesus proclaimed the "gospel," or the "good news," of the kingdom. Rather than doing away with the law, Jesus taught that he was the fulfillment of the law (Matthew 5:17). But obedience to the law was different from what the religious leaders had taught and

practiced. Instead of practicing righteousness in ways that others could see, Jesus said that God valued those who obeyed him secretly in order to be rewarded by him. Instead of focusing on outward forms of worship and outward purity, Jesus taught the people to prioritize worship of God that flowed in purity from the heart.

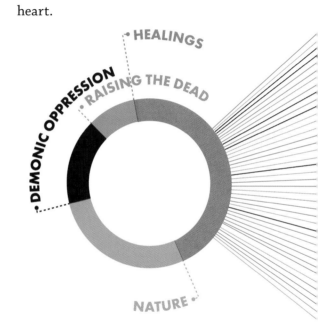

Jesus taught that the kingdom of God had massive implications for the way we approach life. Instead of trying to store up treasures on earth, we ought to give generously and store up treasures in heaven. Instead of preserving our lives on earth and ultimately losing them in death, we ought to sacrifice our lives on earth for

MIRACLES

Jesus healed Peter's mother-in-law of a fever by touching her hand • Matthew 8:14–15

Jesus rebuked the wind and the raging sea and caused them to be calm • Matthew 8:23–27

Jesus cast a legion of demons out of two men and let the demons go into a herd of pigs • Matthew 8:28–34

Jesus drove out demons with his word • Matthew 8:16

Jesus healed a paralyzed man and also forgave his sins • Matthew 9:1–8

Jesus healed a woman suffering from bleeding when she touched the hem of Jesus' garment • Matthew 9:20–22

Jesus raised Jairus's daughter from the dead • Matthew 9:23–25

Jesus healed two blind men when he touched their eyes • Matthew 9:27–30

Jesus healed a mute demoniac, and then the man was able to speak • Matthew 9:32–33

Jesus healed a man who had a shriveled hand • Matthew 12:10–13

Jesus drove a demon out of a blind and mute man, who was then able to speak and to see • Matthew 12:22

Jesus fed five thousand-plus people with five loaves and two fish • Matthew 14:15–21

Jesus walked on the water of a raging sea • Matthew 14:25

Jesus made it possible for Peter to walk on the water • Matthew 14:28–31

Jesus healed the lame, the blind, the crippled, and the mute • Matthew 15:30–31

Jesus cast a demon out of a Canaanite woman's daughter without even going to her • Matthew 15:22–28

Jesus fed four thousand men plus women and children with seven loaves and a few fish • Matthew 15:32–39

Jesus was transfigured • Matthew 17:1–9

Jesus drove a demon out of a young boy • Matthew 17:14–18

Jesus sent Peter to catch a fish with money in its mouth so Peter could pay the temple tax • Matthew 17:24–27

Jesus healed two blind men by the roadside by touching their eyes • Matthew 20:30–34

Jesus healed the blind and the lame in the temple • Matthew 21:14

Jesus cursed a fig tree and thus caused it to wither and die very quickly • Matthew 21:17–20

Jesus was resurrected • Matthew 28:5–10

Jesus healed a deaf and mute man in the region of the Decapolis • Mark 7:31–35

Jesus healed a blind man at Bethsaida by spitting on his eyes • Mark 8:22–26

Jesus walked right through a crowd that was trying to throw him off a cliff • Luke 4:29–30

Jesus drove out an unclean demon from a man in a synagogue • Luke 4:33–36

Jesus caused Peter to make a great catch of fish, which filled two boats • Luke 5:4–11

Jesus brought to life the dead son of the widow of Nain • Luke 7:11–15

Jesus healed a woman who was bent over and couldn't straighten up • Luke 13:11–13

Jesus healed a man of abnormal swelling in the house of a prominent Pharisee • Luke 14:1–4

Jesus healed ten lepers at the same time • Luke 17:11–19

Jesus healed the ear of Malchus after Peter struck it off with a sword • Luke 22:50–51

Jesus turned water into wine • John 2:1–11

Jesus healed a royal official's son of a fever • John 4:46–54

Jesus healed a man at the pool of Bethesda who had been sick for thirty-eight years • John 5:2–9

Jesus healed a man who was born blind • John 9:1–7

Jesus raised Lazarus from the dead • John 11:41–44

Jesus caused the disciples to make a miraculous catch of fish • John 21:3–11

WHAT WAS THE PURPOSE OF THE MIRACLES?

TO SHOW COMPASSION   •   **TO SHOW DIVINITY**   •   **TO FORESHADOW THE KINGDOM**

Jesus and find eternal life in him. Instead of seeking glory and praise from other people, we ought to pursue God's glory and receive our praise from him.

Jesus not only taught about the kingdom and proclaimed the gospel; he was also the embodiment of the kingdom and the gospel. From the beginning of his life through his death, Jesus worshiped God perfectly from the heart, gave his life for others, and pursued God's glory rather than caring about the opinions of other people.

THE DEATH OF JESUS

But Jesus did not come just to perform miracles and teach about the kingdom. In fact, Jesus says the main reason he came to earth was to die (John 12:27). Without Jesus dying for the sins of the people, there would be no good news.

As Jesus approaches the final days of his ministry, he begins to speak to his disciples about his coming death: "We are going up to Jerusalem . . . and the Son of Man will be delivered over to the chief priests and the teachers of the law. They will condemn him to death and will hand him over to the Gentiles, who will mock him and spit on him, flog him and kill him. Three days later he will rise" (Mark 10:33–34).

The disciples have a difficult time understanding what Jesus means until he shows them more clearly during his last meal with them. At this final meal, Jesus shifts the focus of the meal to speak about himself and what is soon to come. Before passing out the bread, Jesus says to them, "This is my body given for you; do this in remembrance of me" (Luke 22:19). And before passing around the cup, he says to them, "This cup is the new covenant in my blood, which is poured out for you" (Luke 22:20). Jesus is telling them that by being broken in his death for them, he is like the Passover lamb. Just as God delivered his people from slavery by the blood of the lamb, Jesus will deliver his people from sin by his own blood. Those who believe in him are saved by his broken body and poured-out blood. But this sacrifice is different, because it establishes the new covenant promised by the prophets. Those who believe in Jesus will be saved and brought back to God forever.

Under pressure from the religious leaders, one of the disciples, Judas, betrays

THE PASSION WEEK

Time	Event	Day	MATTHEW	MARK	LUKE	JOHN	LOCATION
	TRIUMPHAL ENTRY INTO JERUSALEM	SUN	21:1-11	11:1-10	19:29-44		MOUNT OF OLIVES
	JESUS LOOKS AROUND THE TEMPLE			11:11			JERUSALEM
	JESUS RETURNS TO BETHANY			11:11			BETHANY
	JESUS CURSES THE BARREN FIG TREE	MON	21:18-19	11:12-14			MOUNT OF OLIVES
	JESUS CLEANSES THE TEMPLE		21:12-13	11:15-18	19:45-48		JERUSALEM
	CERTAIN GREEKS ASK TO SEE JESUS					12:20-35	
	JESUS REBUKES UNBELIEF					12:37-50	
	JESUS RETURNS TO BETHANY			11:19			BETHANY
	DISCIPLES SEE THE FULLY WITHERED FIG TREE	TUE	21:19-22	11:20-26	21:37-38		MOUNT OF OLIVES
	JESUS' AUTHORITY QUESTIONED BY LEADERS		21:23-27	11:27-33	20:1-8		JERUSALEM
	PARABLE OF THE TWO SONS		21:28-32				
	PARABLE OF THE TENANTS		21:33-46	12:1-12	20:9-19		
	PARABLE OF THE WEDDING BANQUET		22:1-14				
	PHARISEES' QUESTION ABOUT PAYING TAXES		22:15-22	12:13-17	20:20-26		
	PHARISEES' QUESTION ABOUT THE RESURRECTION		22:23-33	12:18-27	20:27-40		
	QUESTION ABOUT THE GREAT COMMANDMENT		22:35-40	12:28-34			
	JESUS' QUESTION ABOUT DAVID'S LORD		22:41-46	12:35-37	20:41-44		
	WOE TO THE TEACHERS OF THE LAW AND PHARISEES		23:1-39	12:38-40	20:45-47		
	POOR WIDOW'S COINS			12:41-44	21:1-4		
	PROPHECY – DESTRUCTION OF JERUSALEM, LORD'S COMING		24:1-51	13:1-37	21:5-36		MOUNT OF OLIVES
	PARABLES – TEN VIRGINS, BAGS OF GOLD, SHEEP AND GOATS		25:1-46				
	SANHEDRIN PLOT TO KILL JESUS	WED	26:3-5	14:1-2	22:1-2		JERUSALEM
	JUDAS AGREES TO BETRAY JESUS		26:14-16	14:10-11	22:3-6		
	PREPARATION FOR THE PASSOVER	THU	26:17-19	14:12-16	22:7-13		
6:00 PM	JESUS & THE DISCIPLES ASSEMBLE FOR THE PASSOVER		26:20	14:17	22:14-16	13:1	
	DISCIPLES ARGUE OVER WHO IS THE GREATEST				22:24-30		
	JESUS WASHES THE DISCIPLES' FEET					13:2-17	
	JESUS IDENTIFIES HIS BETRAYER		26:21-25	14:18-21	22:21-23	13:18-30	
	JESUS INSTITUTES THE LORD'S SUPPER		26:26-29	14:22-25	22:15-20		
	THE COMMANDMENT OF LOVE					13:31-35	
	JESUS PREDICTS PETER'S DENIAL		26:31-35	14:27-31	22:31-38	13:36-38	
	JESUS GIVES THE UPPER ROOM DISCOURSE					14:1-30	
	JESUS AND THE DISCIPLES SING A HYMN & DEPART		26:30	14:26		14:31	
12:00 AM	JESUS' DISCOURSE ON THE WAY TO GETHSEMANE	FRI				15:1-16:33	
	JESUS PRAYS FOR HIS DISCIPLES					17:1-26	
	JESUS PRAYS IN GETHSEMANE		26:36-46	14:32-42	22:39-46	18:1	MOUNT OF OLIVES
	JESUS IS BETRAYED AND ARRESTED		26:47-56	14:43-52	22:47-53	18:2-12	
3:00 AM	JESUS IS BROUGHT BEFORE ANNAS					18:13-14	JERUSALEM
	JESUS IS BROUGHT BEFORE CAIAPHAS					18:24	
	JESUS IS CONDEMNED & MISTREATED THROUGH THE NIGHT		26:57-68	14:53-65	22:54-72		
	PETER DISOWNS JESUS THREE TIMES		26:58-75	14:54-72	22:54-62	18:15-27	
	SANHEDRIN FORMALLY CONDEMN JESUS		27:1	15:1	22:66-71		
	JUDAS GOES OUT AND COMMITS SUICIDE		27:3-10				FIELD OF BLOOD
6:00 AM	JESUS APPEARS BEFORE PILATE		27:2-14	15:1-5	23:1-7	18:28-38	JERUSALEM
	JESUS APPEARS BEFORE HEROD				23:8-12		
	JESUS APPEARS BEFORE PILATE AGAIN		27:15-23	15:6-14	23:13-22	18:39-40	
	JESUS IS SCOURGED AND MOCKED BY THE ROMANS		27:27-31	15:16-19		19:1-3	
	PILATE CONSENTS TO JESUS' DEATH		27:22-26	15:12-15	23:20-25	19:4-16	
9:00 AM	JESUS IS LED AWAY TO BE CRUCIFIED		27:31-34	15:20-23	23:26-32	19:16-17	
12:00 PM	JESUS ON THE CROSS FOR THE FIRST THREE HOURS		27:35-44	15:24-32	23:33-43	19:18-24	CALVARY
3:00 PM	JESUS ON THE CROSS FOR THE FINAL THREE HOURS		27:45-50	15:33-37	23:44-46	19:25-30	
	MIRACLES ACCOMPANYING THE CRUCIFIXION		27:51-56	15:38-41	23:45-49		
	JOSEPH BURIES THE BODY OF JESUS		27:57-61	15:42-47	23:50-55		GARDEN TOMB
	JEWISH LEADERS SECURE THE TOMB	SAT	27:62-66			19:31-42	
	THE WOMEN OBSERVE THE SABBATH DAY				23:56		AT HOME
	MARY MAGDALENE, JOANNA, & MARY THE MOTHER OF JAMES COME TO THE TOMB AND FIND JESUS RISEN	SUN	28:1-8	16:1-8	24:1-8	20:1	GARDEN TOMB

Jesus and hands him over to be arrested. Jesus is placed on trial, and while no valid charge is brought against him, the crowds persuade the governor, Pontius Pilate, to have him crucified.

Jesus is stripped of his clothes, beaten and flogged, and forced to carry his cross to the place of his crucifixion. He undergoes the worst form of torture and death known at the time as his hands and feet are nailed to a wooden cross.

But in his death, Jesus is not only being rejected by men. He cries out from the cross, "My God, my God, why have you forsaken me?" (Matthew 27:46). In his final breath, Jesus cries out, "It is finished" (John 19:30). On the cross, Jesus was not merely dying the death of a sinner. He was dying for the sins of the people, being separated from God and paying the full price for their sins in their place.

THE RESURRECTION OF JESUS

When Jesus took his final breath and gave up his spirit, it felt like the disciples had suffered their worst defeat. Their beloved Teacher had spent years proclaiming that he was the promised Savior who had come to rescue them and the promised King who had come to reign over a new kingdom. But how could he be a Savior when he could not save himself? And how could the King reign over an eternal kingdom when he had been defeated?

On the first day of the next week, two women who were Jesus' disciples went to visit his tomb. But instead of finding a stone covering the tomb, they were shocked to find it open and an angel sitting on the stone. "Do not be afraid, for I know that you are looking for Jesus, who was crucified. He is not here; he has risen" (Matthew 28:5–6).[2]

Soon, Jesus appears to the women, and eventually to all of his disciples, in a resurrected body, turning their sorrow over his death into inexpressible joy. Just as he had promised, Jesus had carried their sins and defeated death. But he could not remain with them forever. Jesus was returning to the Father, and the disciples would now have a new mission as his witnesses to the world.

DID JESUS RISE FROM THE DEAD?

THE KNOWN FACTS

- JESUS' TOMB WAS FOUND EMPTY.
- JESUS WAS TORTURED AND CRUCIFIED.
- CHRISTIANITY SPREAD LIKE WILDFIRE THROUGHOUT THE KNOWN WORLD.
- MANY DIFFERENT WITNESSES (MORE THAN 500) ATTESTED TO SEEING JESUS AFTER HIS DEATH.
- ALL THE DISCIPLES WERE TORTURED FOR THEIR FAITH, AND 11 OF THE 12 ENDED UP DYING FOR IT.
- PREVIOUSLY SCARED DISCIPLES WERE ONLY DAYS LATER CLAIMING THE RESURRECTION WITH BOLDNESS.
- THE DISCIPLES PREACHED TO CROWDS OF THOUSANDS IN JERUSALEM, CLAIMING THAT JESUS HAD RISEN FROM THE DEAD.

THE BEST THEORIES EXPLAINING THE FACTS

1 SWOON
JESUS DIDN'T ACTUALLY DIE, BUT FAINTED (SWOONED) ON THE CROSS AND LATER REVIVED.

2 HALLUCINATION
JESUS' FOLLOWERS ONLY IMAGINED THAT THEY SAW HIM.

3 SPIRITUAL RESURRECTION
JESUS ONLY ROSE FROM THE DEAD IN A SPIRITUAL SENSE.

4 THEFT
THE DISCIPLES STOLE THE BODY AND CLAIMED HE ROSE FROM THE DEAD.

5 WRONG TOMB
CONFUSED BY GRIEF, THE DISCIPLES WENT TO THE WRONG TOMB.

THE MOST PLAUSIBLE EXPLANATION OF ALL THE FACTS IS THAT GOD RAISED JESUS FROM THE DEAD!

OBJECTIONS

- Roman soldiers, who were expert executioners, oversaw the crucifixion and pronounced him dead.
- How could Jesus, after being tortured, crucified, speared, and buried, unwrap himself, move a stone, defeat soldiers, and walk seven miles?
- On multiple occasions and under various circumstances, different individuals and groups of people experienced appearances of Jesus raised from the dead.
- The original disciples believed that Jesus was raised from the dead despite every predisposition to the contrary.
- The gospels claim to be historical accounts, not symbolism or allegory.
- The gospels provide multiple, independent attestations of these appearances.
- The earliest Jewish allegation that the disciples had stolen Jesus' body (Matthew 28:11–15) shows that the body was in fact missing from the tomb.
- The disciples were devastated by the death of Jesus.
- To steal the body, the disciples would have needed an elaborate plan, including bribed guards, sufficient motive, a place to dispose of the body, faked witnesses—all with each of them taking the secret to his grave.
- The story is simple and lacks signs of legendary embellishment.
- Multiple witnesses saw where Jesus was laid.
- If Jesus was only raised in a spiritual sense, what happened to his physical body?
- Jesus' glorified resurrected body still has physical features: he could eat and be touched.
- Paul claims Christianity is pointless without a bodily resurrection.
- There is no evidence that the body was stolen.
- Would the disciples allow themselves to be martyred for an elaborate hoax?
- Joseph of Arimathea's involvement and testimony must be rejected to accept this view.
- If the disciples accidentally went to the wrong tomb, all anyone would have had to do is produce Jesus' body.
- Contemporary scholars have almost universally discounted all these theories. None of these naturalistic theories succeed in meeting the conditions as well as the resurrection theory does.

CHAPTER FIFTEEN

PENTECOST

CHURCH

CONTINUATION OF
JESUS

Even after seeing the resurrected Jesus, the disciples still didn't quite understand what Jesus had come to do and what his plan was for the world. As the story picks up in the book of Acts, the disciples still think that Jesus will bring immediate political victory to Israel. They asked him, "Lord, are you at this time going to restore the kingdom to Israel?" (Acts 1:6). Seeing that Jesus had the power to defeat death, they knew he could easily bring about the defeat of all of Israel's enemies.

But Jesus had different plans. Instead of immediately restoring the kingdom to Israel, he told the disciples he would empower them to spread the good news of the kingdom of God to all nations. "You will receive power when the Holy Spirit comes on you; and you will be my witnesses in Jerusalem, and in all Judea and Samaria, and to the ends of the earth" (Acts 1:8). The same power that fueled Jesus' ministry, the same power with which God had raised Jesus from the dead, would now clothe the disciples so they could spread the good news about Jesus to the rest of the earth. Through the disciples, Jesus was going to gather his people from all over the nations.

The disciples couldn't do this on their own. Instead of laying out specific strategies or providing a precise plan of action, Jesus instructed them to wait in Jerusalem for the promised Holy Spirit.

THE DISCIPLES' PENTECOST

After Jesus ascended to heaven, the disciples did all they knew to do: they prayed. "They all joined together constantly in prayer, along with the women and Mary the mother of Jesus, and with his brothers" (Acts 1:14).

On the day of the Jewish festival of Pentecost, the disciples were still there, praying and seeking the Lord, waiting for the fulfillment of his promise. And then God answered. "Suddenly a sound like the blowing of a violent wind came from heaven and filled the whole house where they were sitting. They saw what seemed to be tongues of fire that separated and came to rest on each of them. All of them were filled with the Holy Spirit and began to speak in other tongues as the Spirit enabled them" (Acts 2:2–4).

The men who had gathered in Jerusalem from foreign countries heard their native tongues coming out of the mouths of the disciples. In awe of the miracle happening before them, a crowd begins to form around the disciples. And just as Jesus had promised, the Holy Spirit emboldened the disciples to be witnesses to the good news of Jesus.

Peter, who had once denied Jesus in front of a few people, now stood in the power of the Spirit to proclaim Jesus to an entire crowd. He recounted God's promise to bring a new covenant and told of how Jesus fulfilled all of God's promises. He boldly charged the people with the

After one Spirit-filled sermon, the number of disciples jumped from 120 to 3,000. From that day on, the Holy Spirit gave power to the disciples to preach the gospel effectively, so that "the Lord added to their number daily those who were being saved" (Acts 2:47). This growing community was in awe of what God was doing, and their awe of Jesus overflowed in sacrificial love for one another. They devoted themselves to the apostles' teaching, to one another, to sharing meals, and to prayer. They shared all their possessions and made sure no one had any need.

DISCIPLES IN JERUSALEM BEFORE PETER'S SERMON

death of Jesus: "This man was handed over to you by God's deliberate plan and foreknowledge; and you, with the help of wicked men, put him to death by nailing him to the cross" (Acts 2:23). Then he called them to repent: "Let all Israel be assured of this: God has made this Jesus, whom you crucified, both Lord and Messiah . . . Repent and be baptized, every one of you, in the name of Jesus Christ for the forgiveness of your sins. And you will receive the gift of the Holy Spirit" (Acts 2:36, 38).

The Lord continued to bless the ministry of the apostles. Wherever they went, signs and miracles accompanied their message, and many Jews believed in each town. When the authorities or crowds tried to silence the disciples, it only emboldened them further. Even the stoning of Stephen, the first Christian martyr, led to the scattering of disciples and further proclamation of the gospel to new places.

A VISUAL THEOLOGY GUIDE TO THE BIBLE

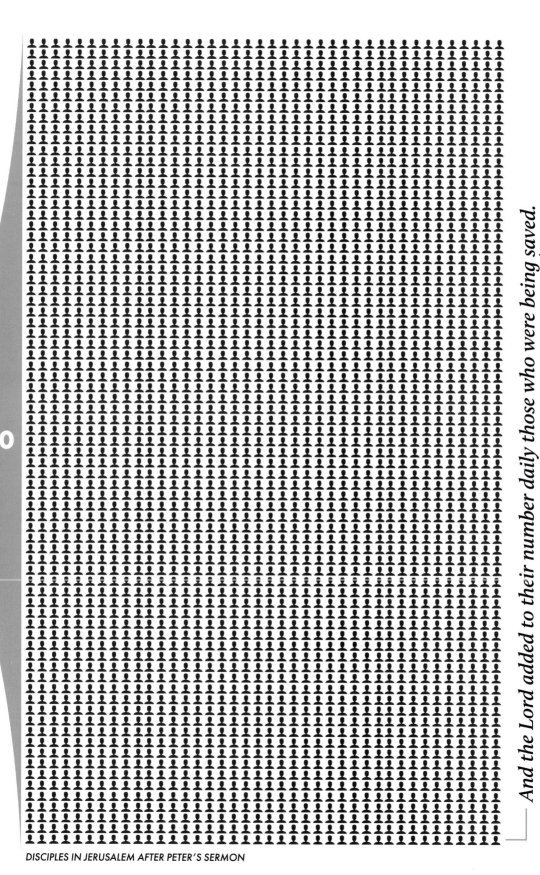

3,000

And the Lord added to their number daily those who were being saved.
Acts 2:47

DISCIPLES IN JERUSALEM AFTER PETER'S SERMON

THROUGH THE SACRIFICIAL DEATH OF CHRIST ON THE CROSS, THE WALL OF SEPARATION HAS BEEN BROKEN DOWN AND HE HAS MADE BOTH JEW AND GENTILE INTO ONE NEW HUMANITY.

GENTILES

JEWS

NOW BOTH ARE PART OF THE KINGDOM OF GOD

THE APOSTLE PAUL

Saul of Tarsus, a zealous Pharisee, was one of the religious leaders who encouraged the stoning of Stephen. Saul believed the growing Christian church was opposed to the will of God, so he went from house to house and dragged Christians off to jail. Widely known for his opposition to Jesus, Saul seemed like the least likely person to be used by Jesus.

But just as God used Moses the murderer, Rahab the prostitute, and David the adulterer, he had plans to use Saul, the chief of sinners, to spread his name among the nations.

While Saul was on his way to persecute Christians in Damascus, Jesus appeared to him: "I am Jesus, whom you are persecuting . . . Now get up and go into the city, and you will be told what you must do" (Acts 9:5–6). As Saul, also called Paul, entered Damascus, Jesus appeared to a disciple in the city named Ananias. He told Ananias to go look for Paul: "Go! This man is my chosen instrument to proclaim my name to the Gentiles and their kings and to the people of Israel. I will show him how much he must suffer for my name" (Acts 9:15–16).

Paul believed in Jesus, was baptized, and immediately began proclaiming the gospel. An apostle of Jesus, Paul carried out a ministry that was accompanied with the signs and wonders of the Holy Spirit, just as the other apostles' ministry had been marked. Much of the last half of the book of Acts tells of Paul's ministry to the Gentiles. From Damascus to Jerusalem to Antioch and across the Mediterranean to Rome, Paul's ministry was characterized by its unsurpassed depth of suffering and its breadth of impact.

THE GENTILE PENTECOST

But there was a problem, a significant shift in the story that had been told up to this point in the Scriptures: How could Paul be an apostle to the Gentiles—to non-Jews? The earliest disciples understood Jesus' message to be for Jews only. Even Jesus had said that he came for the lost sheep of Israel (Matthew 15:24). The Promised King was going to redeem Israel and stomp its enemies under his feet (Psalm 110:1). How, then, could non-Jews be considered a part of God's covenant people?

Like the other disciples, Peter believed the gospel of Christ was for the Jews

SALVATION & THE GOSPEL ARE FOR ALL PEOPLE

Through the sacrificial death of Christ, the wall of separation has been broken down and he has made both Jew and Gentile into one new people of God.

1 GOD'S PLAN FROM THE VERY BEGINNING WAS FOR THE SALVATION OF EVERY PERSON, BOTH JEW AND GENTILE. ▶

2 BEGINNING WITH ABRAHAM, ISAAC, AND JACOB, GOD USED THE NATION OF ISRAEL TO FORM THE ROOT FROM WHICH THIS PLAN WOULD ARISE. ▶

3 WHILE SEPARATING THEMSELVES FROM OTHER NATIONS WITH PRACTICES SUCH AS STRICT DIETARY LAWS, ISRAEL WAS TO BE AN EXAMPLE AND A LIGHT TO THE REST OF THE WORLD TO SHOW HOW MANKIND COULD HAVE A RELATIONSHIP WITH GOD. ▶

4 BEFORE THE MESSIAH CAME, THERE WERE SOME GENTILES WHO RESPONDED TO THIS LIGHT AND FOLLOWED GOD. ▶

5 WHEN GOD SENT JESUS HIS SON AS THE MESSIAH, JESUS PREACHED THAT IT WAS THE HEART THAT DEFILED A PERSON AND NOT WHAT THEY ATE. HE OFFERED HIMSELF AS THE ONE WHO WOULD RULE ON THE THRONE AS THEIR KING. ▶

6 GOD THEN CAST ASIDE THE JEWS WHO REJECTED THE MESSIAH AND GRAFTED THE GENTILES INTO HIS SPIRITUAL KINGDOM. HE USED PETER AND CORNELIUS AS A SPECIFIC EXAMPLE OF THIS NEW UNITY BY INSTRUCTING PETER THAT FORMERLY UNCLEAN THINGS TO EAT WERE NOW CLEAN. ▶

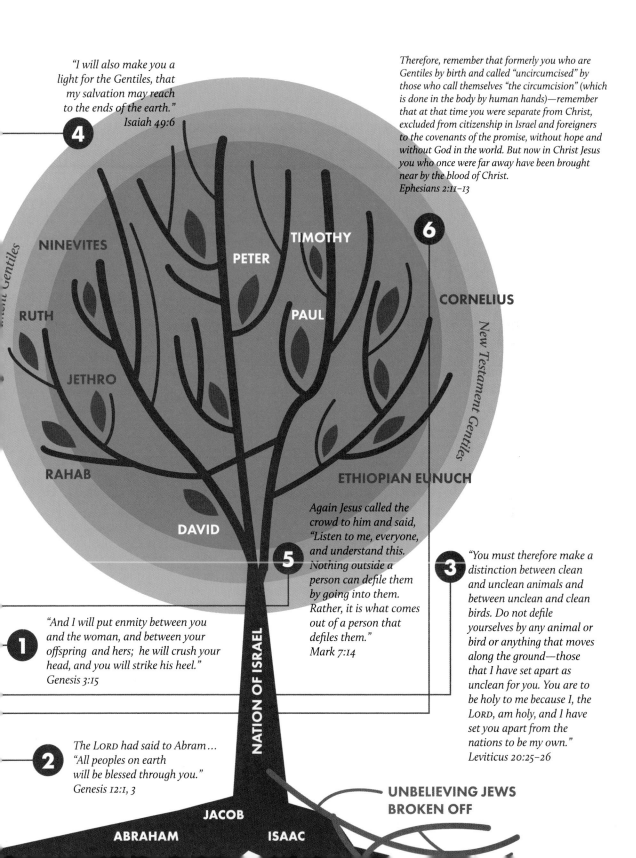

4 "I will also make you a light for the Gentiles, that my salvation may reach to the ends of the earth."
Isaiah 49:6

Therefore, remember that formerly you who are Gentiles by birth and called "uncircumcised" by those who call themselves "the circumcision" (which is done in the body by human hands)—remember that at that time you were separate from Christ, excluded from citizenship in Israel and foreigners to the covenants of the promise, without hope and without God in the world. But now in Christ Jesus you who once were far away have been brought near by the blood of Christ.
Ephesians 2:11–13

6

Gentiles

NINEVITES

TIMOTHY

PETER

CORNELIUS

RUTH

PAUL

New Testament Gentiles

JETHRO

RAHAB

ETHIOPIAN EUNUCH

DAVID

5 Again Jesus called the crowd to him and said, "Listen to me, everyone, and understand this. Nothing outside a person can defile them by going into them. Rather, it is what comes out of a person that defiles them."
Mark 7:14

3 "You must therefore make a distinction between clean and unclean animals and between unclean and clean birds. Do not defile yourselves by any animal or bird or anything that moves along the ground—those that I have set apart as unclean for you. You are to be holy to me because I, the LORD, am holy, and I have set you apart from the nations to be my own."
Leviticus 20:25–26

1 "And I will put enmity between you and the woman, and between your offspring and hers; he will crush your head, and you will strike his heel."
Genesis 3:15

NATION OF ISRAEL

2 The LORD had said to Abram... "All peoples on earth will be blessed through you."
Genesis 12:1, 3

UNBELIEVING JEWS BROKEN OFF

JACOB

ABRAHAM

ISAAC

only. Then one day while he is praying on the roof, Peter receives a vision from God of a sheet descending from heaven with all kinds of animals. A voice speaks to Peter from heaven, telling him to eat, but Peter, knowing that he is forbidden to eat unclean foods, declines the offer. The same voice replies to Peter, "Do not call anything impure that God has made clean" (Acts 10:15).

Next, we learn that the previous day, a Gentile man named Cornelius had received a vision of an angel telling him to send men to invite Peter to come to Cornelius's house. Immediately after Peter's vision, Cornelius's men arrive at the house where Peter is staying and ask him to come with them. While Peter would not typically visit a Gentile home, he knew the vision he had received was from God, and it was leading him to visit Cornelius.

When Peter arrives at Cornelius's home, he preaches the gospel to Cornelius and his entire family. To Peter's surprise, the Holy Spirit falls on these non-Jews, just as the Spirit had fallen on the disciples on the day of Pentecost. Peter is amazed and concludes, "Surely no one can stand in the way of their being baptized with water. They have received the Holy Spirit just as we have" (Acts 10:47). These Gentile believers were baptized and added to the church, thus opening wide the gates for all people to believe in Jesus and to be forgiven of their sins.

The apostles came to understand that Jesus was not only the King of Israel but also the promised Offspring of Abraham, the one through whom God would bless all the nations of the earth. As Jesus had commanded, the gospel was going to the ends of the earth, not to Jewish people alone, but to every tribe and language and people and nation. And as the gospel spread beyond Judea and was received by Gentiles, local churches began to form in every city.[1]

LOCAL CHURCHES IN THE NEW TESTAMENT

ANTIOCH (PISIDIA) • ACTS 13:14; GALATIANS 1:2
ANTIOCH (SYRIA) • ACTS 11:26
ATHENS • ACTS 17:34
BEREA • ACTS 17:11
CAESAREA • ACTS 10:1, 48
CENCHREAE • ROMANS 16:1
COLOSSAE • COLOSSIANS 1:2
CORINTH • ACTS 18:1
CRETE • TITUS 1:5
CYRENE • ACTS 11:20
DAMASCUS • ACTS 9:19
DERBE • ACTS 14:20; GALATIANS 1:2
EPHESUS • ACTS 18:19
HIERAPOLIS • COLOSSIANS 4:13
ICONIUM • ACTS 14:1; GALATIANS 1:2

JERUSALEM • ACTS 2:5
JOPPA • ACTS 9:36,38
LAODICEA • COLOSSIANS 4:15; REVELATION 1:11
LYDDA • ACTS 9:32
LYSTRA • ACTS 14:6; GALATIANS 1:2
PERGAMUM • REVELATION 1:11
PHILADELPHIA • REVELATION 1:11
PUTEOLI • ACTS 28:13–14
ROME • ROMANS 1:7
SARDIS • REVELATION 1:11
SHARON • ACTS 9:35
SMYRNA • REVELATION 1:11
TARSUS • ACTS 9:30
THESSALONICA • ACTS 17:1

CHURCHES OF MACEDONIA
ROME ●
PUTEOLI ●
THESSALONICA ●   PHILIPPI ●
BEREA ●
CHURCHES OF ASIA
TROAS ●   THYATIRA ●
PERGAMUM ●   SARDIS ●
SMYRNA ●   PHILADELPHIA ●   CHURCHES OF GALATIA
ATHENS ●   ANTIOCH (PISIDIA) ●
CORINTH ●
CENCHREAE ●   EPHESUS ●   ICONIUM ●   DERBE ●
LYSTRA ●   TARSUS ●
HIERAPOLIS ●   ● ANTIOCH (SYRIA)
LAODICEA ●   COLOSSAE ●
CRETE ●
● DAMASCUS
TYRE ●   ● CAESAREA
SHARON ●
JOPPA ●   CHURCHES OF JUDEA
CYRENE ●   LYDDA ●
● JERUSALEM

CHAPTER SIXTEEN

APOSTLES

EXILES

THE END

THE COMMANDS OF JESUS AND CONSUMMATION IN JESUS

As the gospel spread to the ends of the earth, just as Jesus had promised, the apostles appointed pastors in each town to oversee the formation of the local churches. As the apostles traveled to preach the gospel, they stopped by these churches and encouraged them. But with the churches spread out across the world, the apostles could only visit them on rare occasions. To continue providing guidance and direction to the growing communities of Jesus followers, the apostles penned letters under the authority of the Holy Spirit. These letters circulated around the churches and taught the believers how to live as kingdom people in the midst of a sinful world.[1]

PAUL'S LETTERS

It's impossible to overstate the breadth of wisdom and insight contained in the letters of the apostle Paul. The man whom Jesus appointed as his "chosen instrument" (Acts 9:15) wrote within the New Testament a letter to the Roman church; two letters to the Corinthian church; one letter each to the church at Galatia, Ephesus, Colossae, and Philippi; two letters to the church at Thessalonica; two letters to Timothy; one letter to Titus; and one letter to Philemon. In these letters, the apostle explores the gospel that was given to him and how Christians ought to live in response to the gospel.

In Galatians 1, Paul explains that the gospel he preached was not his invention, but instead he received it directly from Jesus Christ by a revelation. The gospel preached by Paul was fully in line with the gospel preached by Jesus and the other apostles. What was this gospel? Paul explains in Romans 3:22–25: "There is no difference between Jew and Gentile, for all have sinned and fall short of the glory of God, and all are justified freely by his grace through the redemption that came by Christ Jesus. God presented Christ as a sacrifice of atonement, through the shedding of his blood—to be received by faith."

Paul taught that all of humanity has sinned against God and fallen short of God's glory and his standard for righteousness. Therefore, God had sent his Son, Jesus, to bear the penalty of sin and wrath for our sins and then to rise from the dead, declaring his defeat of death and breaking the curse of Adam. Those who believe in Jesus as Lord are made

SALVATION VIA THE ROMANS ROAD

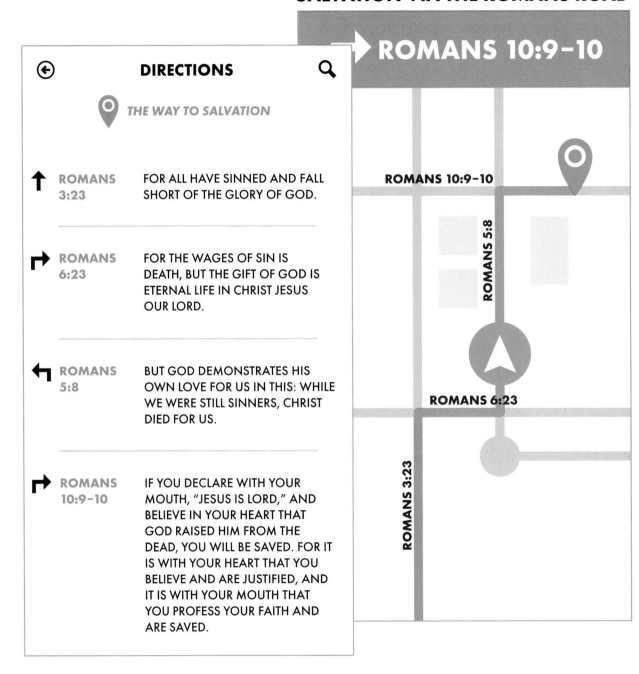

ROMANS 10:9-10

DIRECTIONS

THE WAY TO SALVATION

ROMANS 3:23
FOR ALL HAVE SINNED AND FALL SHORT OF THE GLORY OF GOD.

ROMANS 6:23
FOR THE WAGES OF SIN IS DEATH, BUT THE GIFT OF GOD IS ETERNAL LIFE IN CHRIST JESUS OUR LORD.

ROMANS 5:8
BUT GOD DEMONSTRATES HIS OWN LOVE FOR US IN THIS: WHILE WE WERE STILL SINNERS, CHRIST DIED FOR US.

ROMANS 10:9-10
IF YOU DECLARE WITH YOUR MOUTH, "JESUS IS LORD," AND BELIEVE IN YOUR HEART THAT GOD RAISED HIM FROM THE DEAD, YOU WILL BE SAVED. FOR IT IS WITH YOUR HEART THAT YOU BELIEVE AND ARE JUSTIFIED, AND IT IS WITH YOUR MOUTH THAT YOU PROFESS YOUR FAITH AND ARE SAVED.

ROMANS 10:9-10

ROMANS 5:8

ROMANS 6:23

ROMANS 3:23

righteous by faith as a gift through trusting Jesus and his promises.

Believers in Jesus are children of God, a holy people, brothers and sisters in Christ, citizens of heaven, and heirs of the kingdom. So how should heirs of the kingdom of God live in the world? We ought to love one another as Christ loved us, bear with others' weaknesses as Christ has done for us, carry each other's burdens, and display the fruit of walking in the Holy Spirit: love, joy, peace, patience, kindness, goodness, faithfulness, gentleness, and self-control. We ought to rejoice and give thanks in all things, even suffering, because God is using all things to make us like himself and prepare us for eternity.

Paul not only instructs the churches through his letters but also sets an example for the believers through his life. Paul saw his ministry as "filling up what is lacking in Christ's afflictions for the sake of his body, that is, the church" (Colossians 1:24 ESV). In other words, he wanted to provide a living demonstration of the sacrificial love of Christ to his people. And Paul certainly did this. Just as Jesus gave himself for others' sake, Paul spent himself for the church; just as

Jesus lost his life for others' benefit, Paul lost all things throughout his ministry; and just as Jesus did all of it joyfully for the glory of God, Paul considered all that he lost to be "gain" for the sake of knowing Jesus more (Philippians 3:8–9).

THE GENERAL EPISTLES

In addition to Paul's letters, we have letters known as Hebrews; James; 1 and 2 Peter; 1, 2, and 3 John; and Jude. All of these were written and preserved for us in the New Testament canon.

While the author of Hebrews is unknown, this letter has long been recognized as divine Scripture. It emphasizes Jesus' role as the High Priest of the new covenant who, once for all, made atonement for the sins of the people and sits at the right hand of God. In light of Jesus' example and others who have walked by faith in God's promises, we ought to shed all that weighs us down and faithfully run the race and follow in the footsteps of Jesus.

James's letter has often been called the "Proverbs of the New Testament" for its practical wisdom for everyday life. Along with the other apostles, James begins his letter by encouraging disciples about

THE NEW TESTAMENT LETTERS

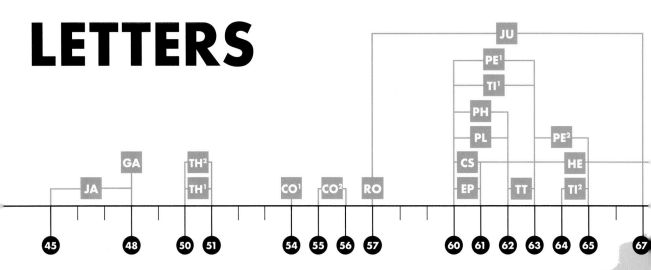

— Authors & Recipients —

James

JA	Unknown

Paul

RO	Roman believers
CO¹	Corinthian believers
CO²	Corinthian believers
GA	Galatian believers
EP	Ephesian believers
PH	Philippian believers
CS	Colossian believers
TH¹	Thessalonian believers
TH²	Thessalonian believers
TI¹	Timothy (ministry associate in Ephesus)
TI²	Timothy (ministry associate in Ephesus)
TT	Titus (ministry associate in Crete)
PL	Philemon (coworker of Paul)

Peter

PE¹	Believers in northern Asia Minor
PE²	Believers in northern Asia Minor

John

JN¹	Believers in Ephesus & surrounding areas
JN²	A church in the region of Ephesus
JN³	Gaius (ministry coworker)

Jude

JU	Unknown

Unknown

HE	Believers in Rome?

Date of Writing

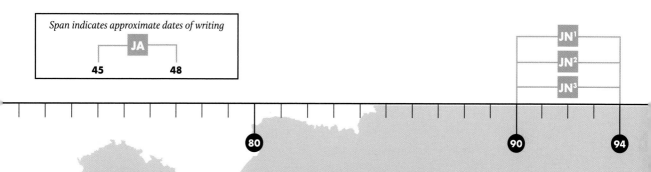

Span indicates approximate dates of writing

JA

45   48

JN¹

JN²

JN³

80   90   94

Location of Writing

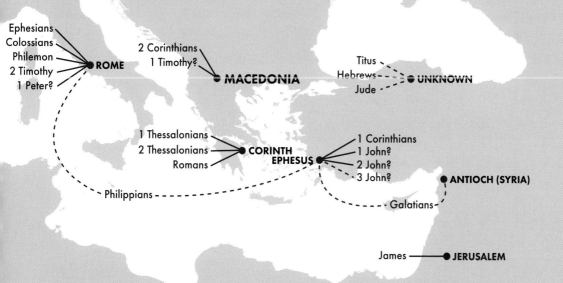

Ephesians
Colossians
Philemon
2 Timothy
1 Peter? ● ROME

2 Corinthians
1 Timothy? ● MACEDONIA

Titus
Hebrews --- ● UNKNOWN
Jude

1 Thessalonians
2 Thessalonians ● CORINTH
Romans   EPHESUS ●

1 Corinthians
1 John?
2 John?
3 John?

● ANTIOCH (SYRIA)

Philippians - - -

Galatians

James ———— ● JERUSALEM

God's purposes in the midst of their suffering. He emphasizes having a living faith full of good deeds, which affects all of life. We ought to live out our faith by being doers of the Word, providing for the needy, guarding our tongues, promoting peace, and submitting ourselves to God.

Peter's first letter is aimed at encouraging the believers in the midst of suffering and telling them how to live as foreigners and exiles in the midst of the world. They ought to walk in holiness, as God's beloved children, and do good in the world. If they suffer for doing good, they are blessed, just like Jesus, who, though innocent, endured suffering on our behalf. In Peter's second letter, he exhorts the believers to grow in spiritual maturity and warns them against false teachers.

The overriding theme of love is the topic of John's three letters to the churches. In light of God's love for us, we ought to love one another, and we demonstrate whether we are truly God's people by the way we love one another. John tells the church how to discern whether they belong to God. God's people love the truth, love one another, love the light, and love righteous living.

Finally, the epistles close with a short letter from Jude, Jesus' half brother. Jude warns the people against false teachers who seek their own gain and deny Jesus. Instead of listening to false teachers, God's people should encourage one another in the Spirit and persevere in faithfulness, trusting that God will keep them until the very end.

THE END

The final book of the Bible is Revelation, a series of visions given to the apostle John about the kingdom of God. At the beginning of the book, Jesus gives instructions and warnings to seven churches. He commends those who have withstood suffering and remained faithful, and he sharply warns those whose love for him has waned and whose love for the world has grown. Then John shows us a vision of the throne in heaven, where all of the heavenly creatures and the host of angels and saints are praising God. The Lamb of God, Jesus Christ, is given all blessing and honor and glory, as every tribe and language and people and nation ransomed by him shout their praise to him.

John utilizes visions and prophetic imagery to show how the kingdom of God, which Jesus began, will be consummated when he returns. In that day, we will be able to say, "Look! God's dwelling place is now among the people, and he will dwell with them. They will be his people, and God himself will be with them and be their God. He will wipe every tear from their eyes. There will be no more death or mourning or crying or pain, for the old order of things has passed away" (Revelation 21:3–4). In that day, Jesus makes all things new and brings about a new heaven and a new earth where God's people dwell with him forever.

The book of Revelation shows us how the story ends with a never-ending kingdom of unhindered joy in the presence of God. Every promise God has made is fulfilled; the promises to Adam and Abraham and Jacob and David come gloriously true. The Seed of Eve, the Offspring of Abraham, the King of David, the Suffering Servant, and the Lamb of God reigns forever and ever. All of this is sure to come, and it is coming soon. "He who testifies to these things says, 'Yes, I am coming soon.' Amen. Come, Lord Jesus!" (Revelation 22:20).

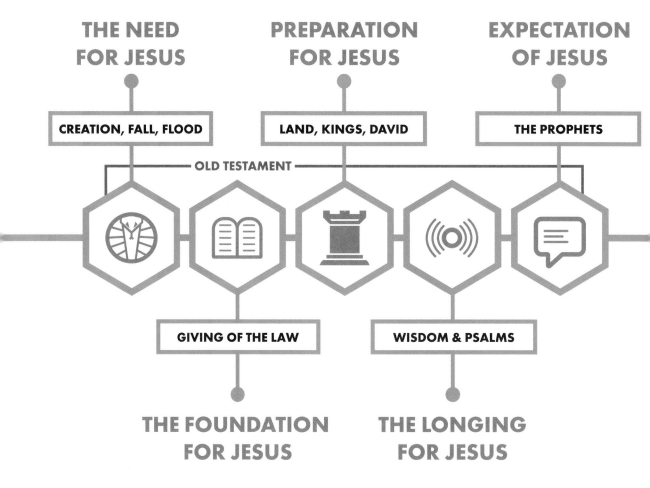

THE NEED
FOR JESUS

PREPARATION
FOR JESUS

EXPECTATION
OF JESUS

CREATION, FALL, FLOOD

LAND, KINGS, DAVID

THE PROPHETS

OLD TESTAMENT

GIVING OF THE LAW

WISDOM & PSALMS

THE FOUNDATION
FOR JESUS

THE LONGING
FOR JESUS

JESUS
COVER TO COVER

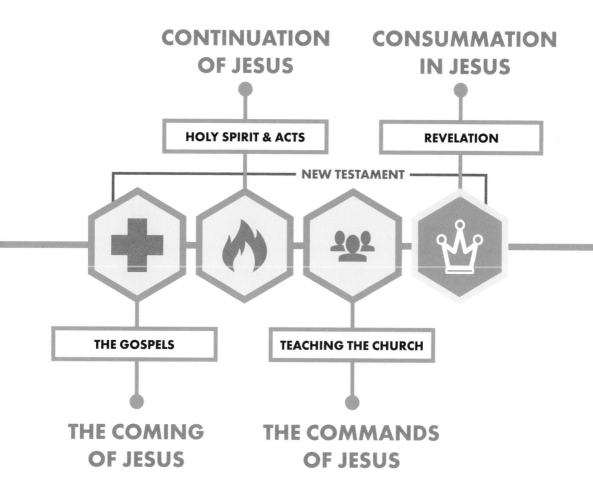

CONCLUSION

We hope this brief journey through the Bible has shown you that the Bible is unlike any other book. It contains everything we need in order to know God, to know who we are and why the world is filled with trouble and pain, and to know of God's plan of salvation in Jesus and how to follow him in obedience. The Bible is clear, written for you to be understood, obeyed, and taught to others. It is authoritative, standing as the Supreme Court of Truth above all other authorities. It is also very necessary, for without it, we could not be in relationship with God or grow spiritually. The Bible is completely trustworthy because it was breathed out by a trustworthy God who never lies.

Jesus is the main character of the Bible's story, and the center of all that is taught and communicated. Creation displays the glory of Jesus. Mankind's fall displays our need for Jesus. The law sets the foundation for Jesus. The prophets proclaim the coming of Jesus, and the gospels reveal the coming of Jesus. The apostles' writings show a world being transformed by Jesus, as his Spirit continued his work and his church reflects his gospel. The end of the Bible shows that all things are culminating in the worship of his name.

Our prayer as we come to the end of this book is that each day you will open the greatest Book—and as you daily trust the Bible and study the Bible and grasp the story of the Bible, that you will join the heavenly host and worship the Hero of the Bible.

ACKNOWLEDGMENTS

We want to thank our wives and children for their support through the production of another book. We want to thank our church families and pastors for their encouragment and excitement for this project. We want to thank the team at Zondervan for their commitment to making this book far better than it otherwise would have been. We want to thank Joey Schwartz for stepping in to carry the load of writing when medical issues prevented Tim from doing it himself. And we want to thank you for reading it.

INTRODUCTION

1. We wanted to start out the book by showing you how important the Bible is to our Western culture and how widespread the use of the Bible is around the world. Fun fact: from the time the infograph was conceived to the time these notes were typed up, the number of full Bible and New Testament translations went up by 13! See "State of the Bible Scorecard," American Bible Society, July 2018, www.americanbible.org/state-of-the-bible-scorecard; "Scripture & Language Statistics 2018," Wycliffe Global Alliance, October 1, 2018, www.wycliffe.net/statistics.

2. Cited in Dmitry Sudakov, "At Age 80 Queen Elizabeth II Enjoys Popularity and Respect," April 21, 2006, www.pravdareport.com/world/europe/21-04-2006/79436-elizabeth-0.

3. Quoted in Steve Coates, "Abraham Lincoln and Sojourner Truth," October 29, 2010, *New York Times* ArtsBeat blog, https://artsbeat.blogs.nytimes.com/2010/10/29/abraham-lincoln-and-sojourner-truth.

CHAPTER 1: WHAT IS THE BIBLE?

1. The "Structure of the Bible" infograph on page 16 is the first graphical indication of the larger message of this book—there is one continuous story of Jesus throughout the Bible. This is represented by the flow of the arrows through the books of the Bible. The blue and yellow colors on the full two-page spread also show you visually the percentage of the OT vs. NT.

2. When you see a number before a book of the Bible, it indicates there are two or three books by the same author or on the same theme. In North America, the number tends to be pronounced as "First John" and "Second Timothy," whereas in other English-speaking areas, it is often pronounced as "One John" and "Two Timothy."

3. John Calvin, *Institutes of the Christian Religion*, vol. 1, ed. John T. McNeill (Louisville: Westminster John Knox, 2011), 35.

CHAPTER 2: HOW WAS THE BIBLE WRITTEN?

1. See Wayne Grudem, *Systematic Theology: An Introduction to Biblical Doctrine* (Grand Rapids: Zondervan, 1994), 74–75.

2. Daniel 2:4–7:28; Ezra 4:8–6:18; 7:12–26.

3. See Norman L. Geisler and William E. Nix, *A General Introduction to the Bible*, rev. ed. (1968; repr., Grand Rapids: Eerdmans, 1986), 326. John Frame notes that this is not certain since Jesus knew the Hebrew Scriptures and may have known Greek (*The Doctrine of the Word of God*, vol. 4 in *A Theology of Lordship* [Phillipsburg, NJ: P&R, 2010], 254).

4. Matthew 27:46.

5. See Geisler and Nix, *General Introduction to the Bible*, 327.

6. Frame, *Doctrine of the Word of God*, 245.

7. See Geisler and Nix, *General Introduction to the Bible*, 405.

8. See Geisler and Nix, *General Introduction to the Bible*, 361.

9. See Geisler and Nix, *General Introduction to the Bible*, 360.

10. See Michael J. Kruger, "Do We Have a Trustworthy Text?" in *The Inerrant Word: Biblical, Theological, Historical, and Pastoral Perspectives*, ed. John MacArthur (Wheaton, IL: Crossway, 2016), 312.

11. See Kruger, "Do We Have a Trustworthy Text?" 313.

12. Kruger writes, "A small number of variants remain where our methodology is unable to reach any definitive conclusion one way or the other . . . But such situations are exceedingly rare. And even when they do occur, they do not materially affect the theology or teaching of the biblical text" ("Do We Have a Trustworthy Text?" 315).

13. The infograph "Has the Bible Really Been Preserved for Us Today?" is a visual representation of the "bibliographical test." If a skeptic rejects the transmissional reliability of the New Testament throughout history, then then they must also consider the translations of other manuscripts of antiquity to be unreliable. In other words, they would have to reject all the knowledge of the classical world. See "The Bibliographical Test Updated," Christian Research Institute, October 1, 2013, www.equip.org/article/the-bibliographical-test-updated.

CHAPTER 3: HOW WERE THE BOOKS COLLECTED?

1. F. F. Bruce, "The Canon of Scripture," *Inter-Varsity* (Autumn 1954), 19–22, https://biblicalstudies.org.uk/pdf/ivp/canon_bruce.pdf.

2. See Wayne Grudem, *Systematic Theology: An Introduction to Biblical Doctrine* (Grand Rapids: Zondervan, 1994), 55.

3. See Eugene H. Merrill, Mark F. Rooker, and Michael A. Grisanti, *The World and the Word: An Introduction to the Old Testament* (Nashville: B&H, 2011), 491.

4. See John MacArthur Jr., *How to Get the Most from God's Word: An Everyday Guide to Enrich Your Study of the Bible* (Nashville: Nelson, 1997), 77.

5. When dating the writing of the books of the Bible, scholars generally agree on the dates after the time of David. One of the main considerations when dating earlier books is to determine events in Judges and when the exodus took place. The infograph "Dates OT Books Were Written" takes a conservative dating approach from Eugene Merrill, placing the exodus around 1446 BC, with the writing of the Pentateuch between then and 1406. See Eugene Merrill, *Kingdom of Priests*, 2nd ed. (1986; repr., Grand Rapids: Baker Academic, 2008).

6. Infographs on the early church canon: F. F. Bruce, *The Canon of Scripture.* (Downers Grove, IL: InterVarsity, 1988); Norman L. Geisler and William E. Nix, *A General Introduction to the Bible* (1968; repr., Grand Rapids: Eerdmans, 1986); Bruce Metzger, *The Canon of the New Testament: Its Origins, Development, and Significance* (Oxford: Clarendon, 1997); see also Grudem, *Systematic Theology.*

7. Quoted in F. F. Bruce, *The Epistle to the Hebrews* (Grand Rapids: Eerdmans, 1990), 17.

8. See Bruce Metzger, *The Canon of the New Testament: Its Origins, Development, and Significance* (Oxford: Clarendon, 1997), 7.

9. John Frame, *The Doctrine of the Word of God*, vol. 4 in *A Theology of Lordship* [Phillipsburg, NJ: P&R, 2010], 139.

10. See Grudem, *Systematic Theology*, 57.

11. See Grudem, *Systematic Theology*, 58.

CHAPTER 4: WHAT MAKES THE BIBLE UNIQUE?

1. See Kevin DeYoung, *Taking God at His Word: Why the Bible Is Knowable, Necessary, and Enough, and What That Means for You and Me* (Wheaton, IL: Crossway, 2014), 44–45.

2. See Wayne Grudem, *Systematic Theology: An Introduction to Biblical Doctrine* (Grand Rapids: Zondervan, 1994), 132–34.

3. Mark D. Thompson, *A Clear and Present Word: The Clarity of Scripture* (Downers Grove, IL: InterVarsity, 2006), 169–70.

4. Grudem, *Systematic Theology*, 73.

CHAPTER 5: CAN WE TRUST THE BIBLE?

1. Timothy Keller, *The Reason for God: Belief in an Age of Skepticism* (2008; repr., New York: Penguin, 2018), 100–17.

2. See Keller, *Reason for God*, 103–4.

3. See Keller, *Reason for God*, 107–10.

4. The infograph titled "Are the Gospels We Have Today Accurate and Reliable?" on pages 64–65 was adapted from J. Warner Wallace, *Cold-Case Christianity: A Homicide Detective Investigates the Claims of the Gospels* (Colorado Springs: Cook, 2013).

5. The date of the prescriptions shown in the "Is the Old Testament We Have Today Accurate?" infograph is unknown, but its roots date to the Babylonian Talmud (source: Samuel Davidson, *The Text of the Old Testament* [London: Longman, Brown, Green, Longmans, & Roberts, 1856], 89).

6. Frank Turek, *Stealing from God: Why Atheists Need God to Make their Case* (Colorado Springs: NavPress, 2014), 174.

7. Albert Einstein, "Physics and Reality," *Journal of the Franklin Institute* 221 (1936): 349–82.

8. Keller, *Reason for God*, 89.

9. Keller, *Reason for God*, 95–98.

10. The infograph "There Is One Story" on page 73 was adapted from Josh McDowell, *The Best of Josh McDowell: A Ready Defense*, compiled by Bill Wilson (Nashville: Thomas Nelson, 1993), 27–28.

CHAPTER 7: HOW DO I STUDY THE BIBLE?

1. Donald S. Whitney, *Spiritual Disciplines for the Christian Life*, rev. ed. (Colorado Springs: NavPress, 2014), 29.

2. John Koblin, "How Much Do We Love TV? Let Us Count the Ways," *New York Times*, June 30, 2016, www.nytimes.com/2016/07/01/business/media/nielsen-survey-media-viewing.html.

3. This is confirmed by LifeWay Research (see "LifeWay Research: Americans Are Fond of the Bible, Don't Actually Read it," https://lifewayresearch.com/2017/04/25/lifeway-research-americans-are-fond-of-the-bible-dont-actually-read-it/). In response to the question "Why have you not read the Bible more?" the number one reason the Americans surveyed gave was, "I don't prioritize it."

4. R. C. Sproul, *Knowing Scripture*, rev. ed. (Downers Grove, IL: InterVarsity, 2009), 20.

5. If you want to go through the Bible in a year, "*The Discipleship Journal* Bible Reading Plan" from The Navigators is a great way to start (see www.navigators.org/wp-content/uploads/2017/04/Discipleship-Journal-Bible-Reading-Plan-9781617479083.pdf).

6. Howard G. Hendricks and William D. Hendricks, *Living by the Book: The Art and Science of Reading the Bible* (Chicago: Moody, 2007), 202.

7. Start by faithfully attending your local church and learning from your pastor's preaching. You can supplement this by listening to the online resources of other sound teachers like John MacArthur, John Piper, and R. C. Sproul.

8. Hendricks and Hendricks, *Living by the Book*, 289–90.

9. Andrew M. Davis, *An Approach to Extended Memorization of Scripture* (Greenville, SC: Ambassador International, 2014).

CHAPTER 8: WHAT IS THE BIBLE ABOUT?

1. The idea of the books of Acts as a continuation of Jesus was inspired by J. D. Greear's *Jesus Continued . . .: Why the Spirit Inside You Is Better Than Jesus Beside You* (Grand Rapids: Zondervan, 2014).

CHAPTER 11: LAND, JUDGES, & KINGS: PREPARATION FOR JESUS

1. Data for sites, regions, and routes on the "Taking the Land" infograph was compiled by Greg Ward for OakTree Software from a variety of scholarly sources. Since some scholars disagree on the details, editorial judgment was often combined with examination of the biblical references and scholarly sources in order to reach a decision. The data is intended purely as a guide and certainly not as an authoritative source in itself.

2. The dates and information for "The Kings & Prophets of Israel & Judah" infograph on page 143 were compiled from Eugene Merrill, *Kingdom of Priests*, 2nd ed. (1986; repr., Grand Rapids: Baker Academic, 2008), and Edwin R. Thiele, *The Mysterious Numbers of the Hebrew Kings*, rev. ed. (Grand Rapids: Kregel, 1983).

CHAPTER 12: SONGS & WISDOM: THE LONGING FOR JESUS

1. Data for the "Psalms" infograph on page 148 was compiled from H. L. Willmington, *Willmington's Guide to the Bible* (Wheaton, IL: Tyndale, 1981).

2. The infograph "The Complementary Union of Marriage" was adapted from the sermon series "Identity Rescripted" by Dr. Mike Augsburger.

3. The infograph "Looking Inward from the Reality of God" on page 153 was adapted from the chart "How God Is Described in Proverbs" in the NIV Life Application Study Bible, page 1011.

CHAPTER 14: THE GOSPEL & THE KINGDOM: THE COMING OF JESUS

1. The infograph "Miracles" on page 175 was created from data in Joel L. Meredith, *Meredith's Complete Book of Bible Lists: A One-of-a-Kind Collection of Bible Facts* (Minneapolis: Bethany House, 2009).

2. The infograph "Did Jesus Rise from the Dead?" on page 179 was adapted from J. Warner Wallace, *Cold-Case Christianity: A Homicide Detective Investigates the Claims of the Gospels* (Colorado Springs: Cook, 2013).

CHAPTER 15: PENTECOST & THE EARLY CHURCH: CONTINUATION OF JESUS

1. Data for sites and regions on the "Local Churches in the New Testament" infograph was compiled by Greg Ward for OakTree Software from a variety of scholarly sources. Since some scholars disagree on the details, editorial judgment was often combined with examination of the biblical references and scholarly sources in order to reach a decision. The data is intended purely as a guide and certainly not as an authoritative source in itself.

CHAPTER 16: THE APOSTLES, EXILES, & THE END: THE COMMANDS OF JESUS AND CONSUMMATION IN JESUS

1. Dates for the writings of the New Testament books in the infograph on pages 194–95 were compiled from David N. Freedman, ed., *The Anchor Bible Dictionary* (New York: Doubleday, 1992); see also Harold Hoehner, *Chronological Aspects of the Life of Christ* (Grand Rapids: Zondervan, 1978).

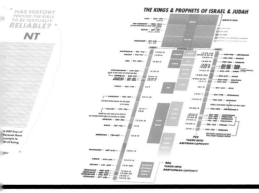
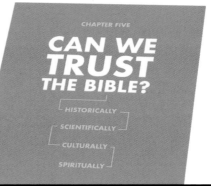

POSTERS • SLIDESHOWS • CLASS NOTES
AND OTHER RESOURCES AVAILABLE AT
WWW.VISUALTHEOLOGY.CHURCH